21世纪全国高职高专旅游系列规划教材

品牌酒店英语面试培训教程

主　编　王志玉

副主编　李领娣

参　编　(按姓氏笔画为序)

丁　蕾　王　正　刘海玲

郭　慧　Mahendra Raj Panday

安　宁

北京大学出版社
PEKING UNIVERSITY PRESS

内 容 简 介

全书分为 5 章。Chapter 1 介绍国际知名酒店(集团)面试的评价标准；Chapter 2 讲述面试中如何进行自我介绍；Chapter 3 为常见的酒店面试问题，该章对面试的问题进行了分类整理，对典型的问题进行了分析并提供了参考回答；Chapter 4 分析了面试中出现的典型错误和不妥行为；Chapter 5 介绍了品牌酒店的各个部门和相关岗位的职责。此外，本书附录为读者提供了面试常用词汇、世界著名品牌酒店集团的基本情况介绍和部分章节的汉语译文。

《品牌酒店英语面试培训教程》是为高等职业院校酒店专业、英语专业学生编写的面试培训教材，同时也适合有志就职于酒店服务和管理的其他专业和社会人士参阅。通过本书的学习和培训，读者可以了解到国内外品牌酒店面试的基本知识，有的放矢地为高端酒店的英语面试做好充分准备，提高面试的成功率。

图书在版编目(CIP)数据

品牌酒店英语面试培训教程/王志玉主编. —北京：北京大学出版社，2011.8

(21 世纪全国高职高专旅游系列规划教材)

ISBN 978-7-301-19029-6

Ⅰ. ①品…　Ⅱ. ①王…　Ⅲ. ①饭店—英语—口试—高等职业教育—教材　Ⅳ. ①H319.9

中国版本图书馆 CIP 数据核字(2011)第 116175 号

书　　名：品牌酒店英语面试培训教程
著作责任者：王志玉　主编
策 划 编 辑：刘国明　李　辉
责 任 编 辑：刘国明
标 准 书 号：ISBN 978-7-301-19029-6/F・2799
出　版　者：北京大学出版社
地　　址：北京市海淀区成府路 205 号　100871
网　　址：http://www.pup.cn　http://www.pup6.com
电　　话：邮购部 62752015　发行部 62750672　编辑部 62750667　出版部 62754962
电 子 邮 箱：pup_6@163.com
印　刷　者：山东省高唐印刷有限责任公司
发　行　者：北京大学出版社
经　销　者：新华书店
787 毫米×1092 毫米　16 开本　10.75 印张　246 千字
2011 年 8 月第 1 版　2017 年 1 月第 4 次印刷
定　　价：22.00 元

序

在经济全球化的大背景下，酒店业正在向国际化不断迈进和发展。酒店业人才的竞争不再局限在本地本国，而是在全球范围内的竞争，跨国就业越来越普遍。

中国旅游高等教育经过几十年的不懈努力，不断为社会培养和输送高素质的旅游人才，这些人才也渐渐成为国际酒店行业竞相争夺的人力资源。近些年来，诸多国际品牌酒店相继来我国组织英语面试，招聘人才，迄今为止我国也已为国际酒店业输送了大批英语和酒店业务过硬的综合型人才。

每一位个体都是一个多面体。

每一位个体都有闪光和优秀的一面或多面。

如何在面试这个舞台上展现自我，把握在品牌酒店就业的机会呢？成功历来是垂青于有实力、有准备，善于抓住机遇的人。

《品牌酒店英语面试培训教程》遵循实用至上的原则，精心研究和梳理国际品牌酒店英语面试的特点、内容和备战技巧，涵盖了面试的方方面面，系统性、针对性强。该书研究了酒店招聘方的经营服务理念、面试标准和面试提问动机，又为应试者的英语语言表达、酒店业务、仪容仪表等各方面能力的展示提供了颇具实用价值的素材和应试策略支持，使应聘者做到知己知彼，为应试做好全方位的准备。从这个意义上讲，该书也是帮助品牌酒店与应聘者相互了解、沟通的桥梁。

当今是一个酒香也怕巷子深的时代。

所以，愿《品牌酒店英语面试培训教程》成为一个摆渡者，在读者细细地品读、学习和练习中，帮助读者沉淀酒香，走出深巷，驶向成功的彼岸。

是为序。

2011年3月

序

前 言

随着我国经济和社会的发展，应用型人才越来越受到青睐。在应用型人才的培养中，高职院校发挥着越来越重要的作用，成为了我国培养应用型人才的摇篮。近年来，高职院校围绕着快出人才、出好人才的目标进行了一系列的改革，人才培养模式由过去单靠院校自身闭门造车式的培养转向了校企合作，贴近市场的新模式，培养出了一批又一批的市场急需人才。

酒店行业是一个劳动力密集型的服务行业。在我国改革开放的大环境下，酒店行业得到了长足的发展。目前，酒店行业的服务和管理水平正在向国际标准化迈进，同时不断提升企业的文化内涵，注入自身发展的文化理念。由此，酒店行业对从业人员的要求也由低素质向较高的职业素质、娴熟的服务技能、开阔的国际视野转变，尤其是近年来，我国境内的高端酒店在招聘面试中增加了对应聘者的英语口语水平的考核。这一趋势反映了酒店行业对人才的需求发生了根本性的变化。

《品牌酒店英语面试培训教程》着眼于学生的职业化教育，帮助欲从事酒店服务与管理的学生走好步入职场的第一步，使学生由读书人更好地向职业人转变。为此，本书在 Chapter 1 中介绍了 4 个国际知名酒店(集团)在我国面试时的评价标准，并根据不同酒店的评价标准，结合近几年其他品牌酒店的情况作了归纳，以便为读者树立一个标杆，有一个准备的目标；在 Chapter 2 中安排了自我介绍，自我介绍是面试中的一个常见的环节，尽管不是每次面试都有，或者自我介绍有长有短，但是，除了申请表上提到的个人情况外，通过这个环节可以展示自己的优势和特点，给面试官留下更加深刻的印象，而且该环节的准备能够为面试的问答环节奠定良好的基础；Chapter 3 涉及面试常见的问题，这一章不仅对常见问题进行了分类整理，而且对面试官提出的这些问题进行了分析，其中着重分析了提出这些问题的动机，尽管本书也提供了一些参考答语，但是更希望读者能根据这些动机，把握回答问题的原则，依据自身的特点，做出相应的回答，而不是死背照搬答案；Chapter 4 列举了面试中常犯的错误及不妥言语和行为，除语言外，还涉及面试时的其他方面，如仪容仪表、肢体语言、目光接触等的注意事项，引以为戒；Chapter 5 重点介绍了酒店的各个部门以及相关岗位的职责。此外，在附录中编排了酒店英语面试常用的词汇，目的是让读者了解或熟悉这些实用的词汇，方便读者在面试中用英语表达。考虑到在国内外都有众多的国际知名品牌酒店，附录还介绍了有关这些品牌酒店的基本情况，作为资料供读者参阅。本书由于是针对英语面试的，故表述的文字以英文为主，旨在通过英文的阅读、学习和训练使读者的准备更加贴近英语环境，更好地适应英语环境的面试。然而，考虑到有些读者的英语水平有限，在附录中提供了部分汉语的译文。尽管如此，仍希望读者尽量不要去看中文译文。为了便于读者自学和练习，我们还录制了模拟面试录音和 Chapter 3 部分问答的录音。

总之，本书具有如下特点。

(1) 实用性强。本书几乎所有的内容都来自于编者多年培训和面试的积累和提炼，全部编写人员均是多年从事品牌酒店面试培训的中外教师，因而提供的资料和内容具有极高的实用价值。

(2) 陈述与分析相结合。既介绍英语面试的知识，又对其进行鞭辟入里的分析。对面试评价标准、自我介绍、注意事项、面试常见提问等方面都进行了独到的分析和讲解，有利于读者真正领会，灵活运用。

(3) 以英语撰写为主。既然是英语面试，我们希望为广大读者提供一个英语学习的条件和机会，使读者学会在面试中用英语表述自己的观点，为真正的面试做好充分的准备。这是本书用英语编写的初衷。

(4) 内容较为丰富、全面。除了语言训练外，还包括品牌酒店评价标准、自我介绍、面试问答、其他面试注意事项、酒店各部门和相关岗位介绍、国际知名酒店基本情况介绍等内容，几乎涵盖了面试的方方面面。

本书可根据不同情况使用。它可以作为高职院校的选修课教材，在学生毕业就业前的一个学期使用，也可以作为培训机构的全日制培训教材，但是建议课程的讲解和实际训练应偏重于后者，即讲解占 1/3 的时间，训练占 2/3 的时间。另外，本书还可以作为其他社会青年自学的参考用书。

本书编写人员分工如下(以章节为序)。

王志玉：Chapter 1、Chapter 4、Chapter 3 部分面试问答录音。

丁　蕾：Chapter 2。

李领娣：Chapter 3。

Mahendra Raj Panday 和长春职业技术学院安宁：Chapter 5、Chapter 3 模拟面试问答录音。

王　正、刘海玲：Appendix A　常用词汇。

郭　慧：Appendix B　世界知名酒店(集团)介绍。

注：部分章节翻译由该章节编写者负责。

全书由李领娣负责统稿。

美国外教 Siebert Charlie 为本书前期的编写提供了部分初稿，山东旅游职业学院的学生为本书提供了照片，谨此表示感谢！

由于编者水平有限，书中难免有疏漏不足之处，诚恳希望读者批评指正，以便今后有机会再版时修正。

王志玉

2011 年 3 月

目　录

目录

Chapter 1

Interview Criteria

What does an interviewer expect from an interviewee? Different hotels and hotel groups have different criteria to assess their interviewees. However, we still can find something in common among their criteria.

For an interviewee who wishes to find a job in a renowned hotel at home and abroad, the primary issue he or she ought to be concerned about is what the criteria of the hotel are. After all, only when you know the criteria or the expectations of the interviewer can you know what you will prepare, so that you will meet the hotel's requirements and succeed in the interview. Only when you are aware of what the interviewer expects from you, can you prepare yourself sufficiently.

It is beneficial to study the assessment criteria, by which interviewers in some renowned hotel groups appraise their interviewees, in order to have a clear picture of this issue.

Here, below, are four assessment sheets given by internationally- renowned hotels while they interview job applicants in China.

1. Hilton Hotel Assessment Sheet

Name: ____________________ Date of Interview: ____________________

Position Interviewed for:________ Nationality: ____________ Age: ________

English

(1) Unacceptable: Cannot answer simple questions, cannot communicate.

(2) Poor: Very basic, poor vocabulary, poor pronunciation.

(3) Average: Able to answer simple questions, basic, acceptable English for rank and file.

(4) Good: Able to communicate with employees and guests.

(5) Excellent: Fluent in English.

Appearance

(1) Unacceptable: Very poorly groomed, poor presentation.

(2) Poor: Needs rigorous improvement.

(3) Average: Needs some improvement.

(4) Good: Groomed up to Hilton standards.

(5) Excellent: Very well groomed.

Confidence

(1) Too shy, insecure to communicate.

(2) Very shy, insecure.

(3) Shy, little insecure.

(4) Confident.

(5) Over confident, close to arrogant.

Education

What kind of education? ______________________________

What level of education? ______________________________

Diploma? Yes/ No

Number of years? ______________________________

Points	English	Appearance	Confidence	Computer Skills
1				
2				
3				
4				
5				

Comments

____

____

____

____

____

____

2. Le Meridian

Interview Assessment Sheet

Applicant's Name: ____________________ Age: ____________________

Position Applied for: ____________________ Date: ____________________

Place of Interview: ______________________________________

Interviewed by: ______________________________________

Rating

(1) Poor (Negative evidence).

(2) Average (Some positive evidence gained. Requires development to perform completely).

(3) Good (Positive evidence gained. Some service behaviors demonstrated).

(4) Very good (Meets all requirements for evidence).

(5) Excellent (Exceeds requirements for evidence).

Assessment Criteria

		1	2	3	4	5
1	Appearance					
2	Voice					
3	Poise					
4	Conversational Ability					
5	Team Focus					
6	Personal Effectiveness					
7	Delivering Results					
8	People Development					
9	Change & Innovation					

Remarks

____
____
____
____

____________________ ____________________________

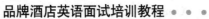

Interviewer's Signature Director of Human Resources

3. Monarch Hotel Interview Assessment Form

Name: ____________________
Date of Interview: __________
Current Position: __________
Place of Interview: _________
Position Desire: ___________
Date Available: ___________
Check the appropriate box in each category. Then make additional comments below.

Points	Appearance	Bearing	Expression	Job knowledge	Motivation	Personality
1	Indifferent to attire & grooming, sloppy	No bearing, lacks confidence, slovenly posture	Uncommuni--cative, confused thoughts, poor vocabulary	None as pertains to this position	None apathetic, indifferent, disinterested	Unpleasant
2	Careless attire, poor grooming	Often appears uncertain, poor posture	Poor speaker, hazy thoughts, ideas	Will need considerable training	Double interest in position	Slightly objectionable
3	Functional Attire, neatly groomed	Holds self well, seems confident	Speaks well, expresses ideas adequately	Basic, but will learn on the job	Sincere desire to work	Likeable
4	Well Groomed	Sure of self, reflects confidence	Speaks, thinks clearly with confidence	Well versed in position, little training needed	Strong interest in position, asks questions	pleasing
5	Immaculate attire & grooming	Highly confident inspires others, asserts presence	Exceptional, speaks clearly, concisely with confidence, ideas well thought out	Extremely well versed, able to work without further training	Highly motivated, eager to work, asks many questions	Extremely pleasing, charming individual
total						

Total Points:

Overall Impression:	Poor	Marginal	Satisfactory	Very good	Excellent
	1～15 points	16～18 points	19～21 points	22～25 points	26 ～ 30 points

Core competencies:
Action Oriented/Adaptability/Communication/Customer focus/Teamwork & Interpersonal skills/Time & Task Management

Comments: ______________________________

Recommendation: ______________________________

Interviewer: ____________________

Date: ____________________

4. Burj Al Arab

Interview Evaluation

Name of candidate: ______________ Date: ________________

Position applied for: ______________ Interviewer: ______________

Rating Scale: 7-Outstanding, 6-Very Good, 5-Good, 4-Satisfactory, 3-Needs Developing, 2-Weak, 1-N/A

Dimension	Rating
Customer Service Orientation The natural desire to help and serve other people. To make the effort to find out what people need and to give to them. This includes customers and colleagues.	
Experience Job knowledge and necessary experience for the position.	
Attitude/Motivation Enthusiasm. Will he/she have a positive affect on colleagues? Self-motivated.	
Appearance Grooming, personal care and attention.	
Team Player Work collaboratively together for the overall benefit of the business. Build good relationships with colleagues.	
Technical Competence Has the necessary skills and technical knowledge for the position. Requires training?	
Communication Skills To relate to guests and colleagues-Up/Down/Across. Confidence. Clarity.	

Continued

Dimension	Rating
Self Confidence Bearing. Assertiveness. Inspires others.	
Potential Probability of candidate developing over time to broader responsibilities & higher position. Demonstrates self-development & self-awareness.	
Personality Likeable and positive. Outgoing. Friendly.	
Overall Assessment/Comments	

To sum up, a job interviewee has to prepare himself in following aspects:

- Appearance
- Oral Communication
- Personality
- Competence

Unit 1.1 Appearance

Firstly, the initial impression an interviewee makes upon a potential employer is by no means unimportant. The interviewer's first sight falls on the interviewee's image. Therefore, professionally-neat grooming and suitable attire is his "name card" to the interviewer. The first judgment the interviewer makes is going to be based on how the interviewee looks and what he wears. That's why it's always important to dress professionally for a job interview.

Secondly, the body language suggests the interviewee's internal world. Proper body language is a helper to sell himself but poor body language is frustrating and is absolutely an obstacle to his success. His poise, eye contact and facial expression reflect whether he is interesting, self-confident or qualified.

Unit 1.2 Oral Communication

It is really a challenge to express oneself in a foreign language. However, keep it in mind that a language is a tool of communication. An interviewer will make it clear that you can exchange your own ideas with him in the foreign language without misunderstanding or abrupt break in the process due to your inappropriate word choice and sentence building or even no words to assist you. Concise and logical statement means a good mastery of the language and clear thinking. So mutual communicating is listed on the top of your priority, which is based on your language skills.

Besides vocabulary and grammar, pronunciation and intonation are factors which influence your oral communication as well. Poor pronunciation and intonation, though not as serious as wrong words and sentences in general terms, will affect the interviewer's judgment negatively. After all, the language of English is one of the items put into his account while an interviewer assesses a non-English native speaker.

In a word, a natural fluent oral language, concise and logical statement and clarified vivid rhythmic voice prove your communicative ability.

Unit 1.3 Personality

The interviewee's personality is another concern of the interviewer, who expects the former's character, temperamental, and mental traits meet the hotel's requirements as an employee.

The traits such as sensitiveness, patience, optimism, outgoing, helpfulness, enthusiasm, confidence, cooperativeness, creativeness are professionally welcome as well as socially pleasing since an employee at a hotel sells his service to his customers. Undoubtedly, this sort of service is characterized by his distinctive quality and behaviors.

Unit 1.4 Competence

Competence is the ability to work. The competence of an employee at a hotel is based on the education he has received and the work experience concerned he has gained. Competence makes it possible to fulfill a particular task at a position. From the education and experience, he obtains necessary knowledge, skills or expertise required for the position he applies for. Therefore, for an interviewer, competence is one of the items in his consideration when he assesses a job applicant.

Questions

(1) How do you present yourself to the interviewers in terms of appearance, oral communication, personality and competence?

(2) What are your advantages?

Chapter 2

Self–introduction

Making a self-introduction will be the first requirement in most interviews. When introducing yourself, do not focus too specifically on any one area. The interviewer will often use the information you give to choose what he or she would like to ask next. While it is important to give an overall impression of who you are, make sure to concentrate on work related experience. Work related experience should always be the central focus of any interview (work experience is more important than education in most English speaking countries). An excellent introduction will make a good initial impression on the interviewer, which will benefit you a lot, as the interviewer considers your application.

Following are some of the ways in which you may be asked to introduce yourself.

(1) Please tell me something about yourself.

(2) Can you sell yourself in two minutes? Go for it.

(3) Could you introduce yourself please?

A good self-introduction should be

Well-organized

Unique

Impressive

What to write

A self-introduction should contain four groups of information—family background, education, work experience and personality. However, you do not have to focus equally on every aspect. It is wise to highlight your uniqueness accordingly.

How to write it

There are four steps.

Step 1: assembling basic information

Step 2: adding extended information

Step 3: including further extended information

Step 4: fitting the introduction created from the first 3 steps into a short and organized one which can be read within 1.5 to 2 minutes

(1) The final introduction should not contain too much information about your family members, where you grew up or what food you like etc., unless it is really helpful in demonstrating your positive qualities.

(2) In the final introduction, there is no need to use any advanced vocabulary to impress the interviewer. Using everyday vocabulary will impress the interviewer more as you will appear more natural and confident.

(3) Do not lie to impress the interviewer. He might focus on the lies and ask for more details, leading to confusion and embarrassment, and the interviewer may discover that you are lying. Hotels want honest employees.

Examples

Following are some examples. It would be helpful to comment on each of them from a job interviewer's point of view. In which way do you think they are persuasive?

Samples

1. Short Sentences Bring Forceful Expression

Good morning Sir/Madam. It's really an honor to be here today. My Chinese name is ***, and you can call me Bruce. I named myself after Bruce lee—the famous Chinese Kungfu star. "Never say die." is Bruce lee's motto, and also mine. I'm always cheerful and ready for the challenges in life.

My major is hotel management. I'm the monitor in my class and a member of the Student Union. These experiences made me a responsible and enthusiastic person.

I'm a huge fan of basketball and a member of the basketball team of our department. I really enjoy the feeling that everyone in the team fight for one goal.

Working in a 4-star hotel gave me the same feeling, and the one-year working experience as a waiter trained me into a flexible and sensitive person.

The hotel industry is highly developed in Dubai, and your hotel is one of the best. It will be a big challenge working in your hotel, and also a wonderful opportunity to improve myself. I will try my best and offer every effort to be a qualified employee.

2. Emphasis on One Character Makes Deep Impression

Good morning Sir. My name is ***, and you could call me George, a freshman majored in hotel management. I'm not the only child in my family, I have a younger sister. When I was a little boy, my father always told me, "You're the brother, so you should take good care of your sister all the time. Remember, you are the man in the family." My father's words always inspire me to take the responsibilities bravely. After I grew up, I tried to seek chances to support my family. I took part-time jobs as a waiter in a local restaurant in my spare time and vocations. It trained me efficient and sensitive to details. After one-year learning in my major, I know better about hotel industry and take it as my long-life career. If I get the opportunity working in your hotel, I'll definitely work hard and never let you down.

More Samples

Sample 1

My name is ______, a 2nd-year student here, majoring in hotel management. I am from Qingdao, Shandong Province. My father runs a small business. My mother is a housewife. I am an only child. I was a good student in high school and my grades were good enough to get accepted at SCTH (Shandong College of Tourism & Hospitality) two yeas ago. Not only have I been maintaining good academic standing throughout my time at the school, but I also have work experience, having worked as a waitress at a Holiday Inn in Beijing two years ago. Overall, I am a hard working student with a strong desire to learn, and I have confidence and the ability to face challenges.

Sample 2

My name is Wang DanDan. People called me Fanny. I am from a not-so-well-do family of 4. My father is a farmer, working 7 days a week and my mother helps my father with his work. As a child, I did well in all subjects in school. My parents made many sacrifices to send me to SCTH to learn so that I will become a professional worker in tourism industry one day. Now I am half way towards reaching my goal. I am very confident that when I graduate I will be able to contribute what I've learned from school to a good hotel. Even though I have no work experience, I am a hard worker and fast learner. I took part in all the major team sports in school. I am well liked by my fellow students and teachers.

Sample 3

My name is ________. I have no English name. I am from Jinan. I went to the best high school in Jinan. My grades are so-so. But through my school years I have been admired by friends and teachers for my ability to solve problems and to organize events in school. I worked hard and took my assignments seriously. My father is a lawyer and my mother is a part-time accountant. From my early childhood, my parents have taught me to be independent and responsible. That is why I earned most of my pocket money myself by doing different jobs while I was in high school and still do so in college.

Sample 4

People call me _______. I am from a small family in Hebei, and was raised by my grandparents. To this day, I still feel closer to them than to my parents. I am not as out-going as others are but I don't see that as a disadvantage because I am a conscientious worker and I get along well with others. I seldom relax until I get my work done well. I am a good organizer. I communicate well with all sorts of people, and I always keep a clear mind. I have a young brother who is in Grade 8. I am the only one whom he looks up to for advice in difficult times, and I am always available when he needs me, as my parents are usually busy with their work.

Sample 5

My name is _____. I am from a family of 5—my parents, my sister (who is married) and younger brother. In a traditional Chinese family the son usually gets the chance to get more education and the rest of the family support him. I had a difficult time in school when I was very young as the condition of my family changed constantly. It has been a long road and I've faced many challenges since my early school years. Right now, I am doing very well at SCTH, thanks to my parents and my teachers who have supported and encouraged me. Last year I was one of the lucky ones to get chosen to work in a world famous hotel in Shanghai. I was commended for good work and was invited to work there when I graduated from SCTH. However, I'd like to work abroad to face bigger challenges so that I can be improved a lot more.

Sample 6

I am honored to participate in this interview. My Chinese name is Wang Mei and my English name is May. Korean is my major, however I am also good at English. I suppose this would be one of my advantages since I can communicate in Korean as well as in English.

I worked for a long time as a waitress in a 3-star hotel. This experience is quite memorable. Although I'm still a student, I have learned the skills, sense of service and the positive attitude needed to fulfill my duties.

I love sports, too. I like playing basketball, swimming and hiking, from which I've benefited a lot. Not only am I healthy, but I've also learned how to cooperate with my teammates and how to work under pressure. I get a lot of pleasure from these endeavors, which are not only fun but fill me with a sense of achievement.

People regard me as optimistic and easy-going. I get along well with them and I have many friends. We help and take care of each other.

I believe that I would continue to make progress at your hotel and at the same time show that my abilities and personality would be valuable to you.

Useful Expressions:

(1) Talking about strong points.

I think my three strongest strengths are details-oriental, patient and communicative.

I think I'm a mature, self-motivated and honest person.

I'm a person of a stable personality, high sense of responsibility and strong interpersonal skills.

I'm a senior of my college with a pleasant mature attitude.

(2) Talking about weaknesses.

I am a perfectionist and I pay very much attention to details. Sometimes I am quite captious.

I have had trouble in the past with scheduling and prioritization. However, I'm now taking steps to correct this.

I think I have to develop my public-speaking skills.

I'm afraid I need to get better at giving presentations and talking in front of others.

(3) I have been doing quite well at college and one of the top students in the class.

(4) Talking about the achievements in college.

At college I won a scholarship and the first prize in a English speech contest.

I've received the honor of the most outstanding student in 2010.

I received the level-10 professional recognition on piano-playing by the National Pianists Association, with 10 being the highest level.

I received first-class scholarship for finishing the year in the top 5 percent of the class.

I achieved the target of ...

I finished the project successfully and witnessed the revenue of ...

(5) I have already learned a lot in the classroom and I hope to be able to make practical use of it in your company. I am sure I can apply what I have learned to the work in your hotel.

(6) I'm willing to work under pressure and have the ability to work well with others.

(7) With my qualifications and experience, I feel I am hardworking, responsible and diligent in any project I undertake.

(8) I'm aware that the position requires highly-motivated and reliable person with excellent health and pleasant personality...

(9) My working experience made me a highly organized and efficient person.

(10) (Talking about how long I'd like to stay in the company once hired) As long as my position here allows me to learn and to advance at a pace with my abilities.

(11) (Talking about the reason of being interested in the interviewer's hotel/company) I read an article in the newspaper and was very impressed by ...

(12) I believe that I can fulfill the requirements in your company...

Questions:

(1) Describe your personalities with 3 words, and explain them one by one.

(2) Talk about your working experience in 3 sentences, trying to include the following points: time, hotel name, position, and what you have learned from this experience.

(3) Try to work your self-introduction out by following the four steps mentioned above.

Categorized Questions & Analysis

Chapter 3

Introduction

The interview is a well-planned project with sufficient consideration and detailed schedules for both interviewers and interviewees. As the old saying goes in China, know the enemy and know yourself and you can fight a hundred battles with no danger of defeat. Consequently, in order to pass the interview and finally get the job offer, interviewees should know well the questions probably proposed, the motives behind those questions, how to answer each kind of question approximately and different kinds of questions in different interviews. This chapter is subdivided into four parts and the above four aspects will be discussed respectively.

Unit 3.1 Categorized Questions

1. Customer Focus

(1) What do you think our customers expect in terms of service?

(2) How can you tell whether a customer is happy or not? If not, what steps can you take to solve his problem?

(3) What would be your reaction if a customer invited you to a nightclub?

(4) Tell me about a time when you had to deal with a difficult customer on your own.

(5) How have you handled difficult customers?

(6) Describe your ideal job.

2. Team Focus

(1) Describe a team or group of which you have been a member recently.

(2) Describe your role within the team.

(3) How effective do you feel your behavior was when you were in a situation where the team members responded positively to you? How about when they responded negatively?

(4) How would your colleagues describe you?

(5) How have others appraised you? How have your weaknesses been perceived by your clients/colleagues/bosses/ subordinates?

(6) What nationalities have you worked with?

(7) When a colleague was in need of assistance, what, where, when and how did you assist? Give an example.

(8) Are you a good team player and why?

3. Personal Effectiveness

(1) What experience have you had in scheduling routines?

(2) What do you see to being the key stages in organizing and completing a project?

(3) Give me an example of how you have taken responsibility for your own learning.

(4) What training needs do you think would help you to improve your career?

(5) What are your limitations at work?

(6) What have you learned from your mistakes?

(7) What inspires you?

(8) How did you improve yourself last year?

(9) Do you work well on your own?

(10) If I were to tell you that I do not like you, how could you change my mind?

(11) What qualifications do you think the job requires?

(12) What makes you better than other candidates?

(13) Do you work well under pressure?

4. Delivering Results

(1) How do you go about prioritizing your actions during the day?

(2) What motivated you to be in this interview?

(3) How do you ensure the standards are implemented in the hotel?

(4) Quality is the prime dimension in the hospitality industry. What would your approach in maintaining quality?

5. People Management

(1) What aspects of your job require you to work with other people?

(2) Can you give me an example of when you have had to solve a problem in your work place or college or family and how did you handle it?

(3) What would one need to do in the event of an argument at work?

(4) What suggestions would you make to have the sale of an Italian restaurant in your city increased over the next 3 months having seen a potential market available?

(5) What is your motivation for applying for this position?

(6) What contribution could you offer to our organization?

6. Education and Employment

(1) How do your studies at school relate to this job?

(2) How did you benefit from your summer vacation work?

(3) Name three things you learned in school that you could apply to this job.

(4) How do you appraise your school, your teachers and your fellow students?

(5) What excited you most at school?

7. General

(1) What do you expect from an organization?

(2) What do you know about our company/ hotel?

(3) What is your remuneration expectation?

(4) Why do you think you are suitable for this job?

(5) What do you see about yourself in about five years? / Tell me about your five-year plan.

(6) Why have you applied for this position in our hotel?

(7) Can you tell me some of the job responsibilities?

Unit 3.2 Interviewers' Motives to Ask a Question

Interviewers always expect to, within a limited period of time, know as much as possible about interviewees and decide whether he/she is the right choice for their hotel. Accordingly, the interview is a comprehensive test of interviewees. As a goal-oriented activity, the interview is quite well-organized, which means interviewers would never question interviewee casually but rather with a definite motive and goal. So interviewees not only have to prepare a resume, a unique self-introduction, for possibly raised questions but most importantly the motives of interviewers. In the following part, the motives will be analyzed in detail with the help of some typical questions.

(1) Q: *Would you please say something about your family?*

This is a very typical question. The interviewer does not intend to know where your hometown is or what your parents do but the influence of family environment on you. Focus on how your parents cultivate your personality and character in a subtle way. Questions of this kind are as follows.

① What kind of personality traits do you admire?

② What kind of people do you like to make friends with?

③ What kind of colleagues do you expect to work with?

④ How would your friends and classmates describe you?

⑤ How would your colleagues describe you?

⑥ If you were an animal, which animal would you choose? Why?

...

The motive involved here is to know what kind of personality you have from your family, friends or your expectation of other people and then decide whether you are suitable for the job. Consequently, state the personality necessary for the position. Do not go far away.

Answer for reference: *There are three members in my family, my parents and me. My father works as a Chinese teacher in a Senior Middle School and he's busy all the year round. He always expects me to take care of myself and to make choices independently. As for my mom, she is kind and honest with neighbors, colleagues and friends.*

(2) Q: *In your spare time, what do you often do?*

Through this question, the interviewer could know about your extracurricular life, but the real motive behind it is to test your English speaking ability and physical appearance. Could you handle everyday topic freely? Could you make eye contact while speaking? Could you wear a smile and use appropriate body language? What's more, make sure to state your answer in a clear and logical way.

Answer for reference: *In my spare time, I often play badminton with friends, read English novels, for example, Jane Eyre, Great Expectations etc, or climb mountains. For me, spare time is necessary and I want to take good advantage of it to enrich my mind and build my body.*

Questions of this kind are as follows.

① *Describe a team or group of which you have been a member recently.*

② *Describe your role within the team.*

③ *What have you learned from your mistakes?*

④ *Would you tell us your greatest failure?*

⑤ *Would you tell us your experience when you were moved/when you made a big mistake?*

⑥ *What kind of books/magazines/TV programs do you like?*

…

(3) Q: *What did you benefit from your summer vacation work?*

The interviewer intends to know about your work experience, which might be necessary for the position you applied for. Therefore, make sure your answer is in accord with interviewer's expectation. What's more, get prepared for follow-up questions, which are commonly asked of this sort of question. For example, *Where/ how long/ what position did you work? What's the most important thing have you learned? Did you meet any difficult customer? How did you deal with that? How did your colleagues/your supervisor/boss describe you? …*

For instance, you apply for the position of waiter, for which sense of service and responsibility are a necessity. Your answer to the above questions then should focus on the requirements to be a waiter.

Answer for reference: *During summer vacation, I worked as a waiter in a three-star hotel in Jinan for more than one month. Sense of service and responsibility are the most important things that I have benefited from it. I should always pay close attention and offer satisfying service to customers from their entry to the hotel to their departure.*

Similar questions are as follows.

① *What do you think our customers expect in terms of service?*

② *Please describe your job duty.*

③ *Describe your ideal job.*

④ *What do you think is the difficult/challenging part in your job?*

⑤ *What suggestions have you made to your hotel?*

⑥ *Can you tell me some of the job responsibilities?*

…

(4) Q: *Why do you want to work for our hotel instead of other hotels in Dubai?*

The motive to ask such a question is to know your motivation and expectation while applying for the job. The most expected answer will always be what you can do for the hotel not what the hotel can do for you. Probably you could improve your English and make more friends in Dubai, but that's not the key points.

Do not state what the hotel can do for you.

Tell what you can do for the hotel.

Fig. 3.1

Answer for reference: *Your hotel, with a spirit of enterprising and openness, plays a leading role in hotel industry. Your management is first-class and progressive. I believe I can make certain contribution to your hotel with my ability and talents.*

In addition, full preparation is a must. Before the interview, try every possible way to collect information about the position applied and the hotel, including its management ideas, distinguishing features, history, location, market assessment and so on.

Questions of this kind are as follows.

① *What motivated you to be in this interview?*

② *Why have you applied for this position in our hotel?*

③ *What do you know about our hotel?*

④ *What is your favorite job?*

⑤ *What kind of leaders do you like best?*

⑥ *What kind of company/hotel do you like? Why?*

⑦ *When you seek a job, which factor counts the most to you?*

⑧ *What contribution can you make to our hotel?*

…

(5) Q: *What do you see about yourself in about five years? / Tell me about your five-year plan.*

As for your career development, you may have made a five-year plan or even a long term plan. Or you haven't any plan for the future, which you should spare some time and make a plan for. Anyway, this question concerns your ambition, confidence and enterprising spirit. Deliver the information of a proper ambition, confidence and enterprising spirit to interviewer through your answer. Do not overdo that.

Answer for reference: *I hope I could become an F&B (Food and Beverage) Supervisor in five years with good professional skills, hard work and satisfactory performance.*

In the meantime, get ready to answer the follow-up questions. For example, how do you plan to achieve that/make it come true?

Questions of this kind are as follows.

① *How did you improve yourself last year?*

② *What is your life-long dream in career development?*

③ *Do you think you can pass this interview? What are your reasons?*

④ *If your boss assigns you a very difficult job, how do you handle that?*

⑤ *Do you have any plan for your career? How will you realize that?*

…

(6) Q: *What is your opinion about doing extra work in the evening or at the weekend?*

The motive to ask this question is to know about your attitude towards job, sense of discipline and honesty or loyalty to your job. Preference will be given to those who obey hotel regulations, keep loyal to the hotel and have a positive attitude towards their job.

Answer for reference: *As far as I am concerned, if there is an urgent need, I will do extra work. I believe the hotel could manage time in a reasonable way and put work efficiency on the priority list.*

Similar questions are as follows.

① *What would be your reaction if a customer invited you to a nightclub?*

② *Do you always try to improve your work efficiency? How?*

③ *Have you ever made proper advice for your school or hotel you once worked in? Please give examples.*

④ *For how many years do you expect to work in our hotel?*

…

(7) Q: *What do you think is the key to success? Why?*

This question is a test of your analytical and judging ability. You are supposed to be able to analyze needs of customers, difficult situations in you job and find corresponding solutions. Try to improve yourself in an all-around way and get yourself ready for the job opportunity.

Answer for reference: *I think the key to success is full of preparation. No one can succeed without any preparation. Success does not come by itself, so we must make good preparation, work very hard and do everything that's needed to seize the opportunity and achieve success.*

Similar questions are as follows.

① *What do you think our customers expect in terms of service?*

② *How can you tell whether a customer is happy or not? If not, what steps can you take to solve his problem?*

③ *What do you see to being the key steps in organizing and completing a project?*

④ *How do you often handle criticism?*

⑤ *If your colleagues misunderstand you, what do you usually do?*

…

(8) Q: *What can you do for us that other candidates can't?*

The interviewer expects to hear your uniqueness compared with other candidates. Indeed, the motive to ask this type of questions is to know whether you really know yourself or have self-control. Knowing yourself completely might be the hardest thing in the world. However, you have to do this. Only when you have a clear picture of yourself, can you know your advantages and uniqueness.

Answer for reference: *I have a unique combination of strong professional skills, and the ability to build strong customer relationships. This allows me to keep more regular customers for the hotel.*

Questions of this kind are as follows.

① *What is your greatest strength and weakness?*

② *If I were to tell you that I do not like you, how could you change my mind?*

③ *If you did not pass this interview, how will you improve yourself later?*

④ *Although you work very hard, you do not make as much money as your colleagues do. What would you do then?*

⑤ *What kind of job do you think you are fit for? Why?*

⑥ *Why do you think you are suitable for this job?*

…

(9) Q: *Are you a good team player and why?*

The interviewer aims to know whether you have a good team spirit or not. Furthermore, by answering this sort of questions, your communicative skills, interpersonal relationships, adaptive and organizing abilities are also tested. In hotel industry, most of the time, team spirit counts more than individual ability, so cultivate your team spirit from now on.

Answer for reference: *Yes, I am. I joined the Students' Council in our department and organizing the recreational and sports activities was my job duty. In order to organize the sports meeting and other activities, I often cooperated with my classmates, designing posters, arranging places and so on. They all enjoy working with me because I always have good ideas and I am very helpful.*

Similar questions are as follows.

① *When a colleague was in need of assistance, what, where, when, and how did you assist? Please give an example.*

② *Do you often talk with strangers? Do you often just talk with your close friends?*

③ *How do you get along with your classmates?*

④ *Which one do you prefer, work by yourself or work with others?*

⑤ *Do you think you are popular and welcome with your classmates? Why?*

…

(10) Q: *How do your studies at school relate to this job?*

This kind of questions is intended to find out your professional knowledge and skills. Prepare for these questions in advance, for instance, get to know the English names of those subjects you have learnt in college and related to the job.

Answer for reference: *I have learnt such subjects as Modern Hotel Management, English for Hotels, Housekeeping Management and so on. What's more, I do the internship for one month in a four-star hotel in our school. All these studies benefit me and prepare me for this job.*

Questions of this kind are as follows.

① *How do you ensure the standards are implemented in the hotel?*

② *Quality is the prime dimension in the hospitality industry. What would your approach in maintaining quality?*

③ *What subjects or courses about hotel have you learnt in college?*

④ *Have you got any certificates about hotel industry?*

⑤ *Do you have any skills for the position of ...?*

⑥ *Tell three things you learned in school that you could apply to this job.*

⑦ *What excited you most at school?*

…

In some interviews, you may encounter such a question form the interviewer, *"Do you have any questions for us?"* Do not haste to ask interviewers about the payment or awards.

It's better to ask questions about the training programs or learning opportunities provided by the hotel, which could reveal your enterprises and that you care more about the job opportunity itself rather than how much money you can get.

Unit 3.3 The Principle of an Answer

Answering questions in an interview quite differs from what you do in class or in daily life. As stated in the above part, the interviewer puts forward each question with a motive and an expected answer from interviewees. Therefore, being aware of how to answer each question is rather important and useful. In order to give satisfactory answers and impress the interviewer, you are supposed to follow several principles, which will be stated in the following part.

(1) Q: *What is your remuneration expectation?*

As for this question, firstly you have to understand the superficial meaning: What does "*remuneration*" mean? If you can not understand it or do not catch it when the interviewer speaks too fast, never answer it based on your own understanding. Ask the interviewer to repeat it or explain it until you can fully get the question. Don't be shy. Answer it as Fig.3.2.

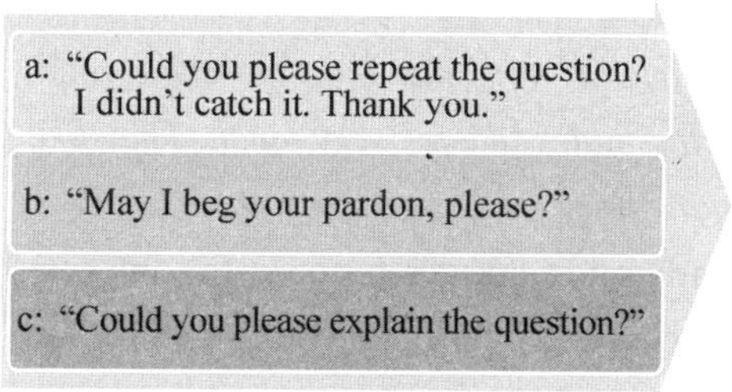

a: "Could you please repeat the question? I didn't catch it. Thank you."
b: "May I beg your pardon, please?"
c: "Could you please explain the question?"

When you do not understand or catch the question…

Fig. 3.2

Secondly, you should take the motive of the interviewer into consideration: why does he/she ask such a question? He/she does not really expect a number from you but your attitude towards salary and work: what counts more?

Answer for reference: *Money is important, but I am still very young and to me, the opportunities and job responsibilities mean more to my career.*

To sum up, the first principle to follow is to understand the question superficially and get the motive of interviewer.

(2) Q: *Why did you choose Hotel Management as your major?*

A: *My parents told me that hotel industry is rising fast with a bright future. There are more opportunities to find a good job when I graduate. So I chose this major. Or, many of my classmates and friends chose this major, so did I.*

If your answer is of this kind, you will definitely impress the interviewer with your lack of dependence, which is totally unadvisable. Interviewers always expect to employ those who can think and work independently.

Answer for reference: *Hotel industry is growing fast and has provided lots of opportunities for those who want to work in this industry. I believe with interest and hard work, I can do well both in college and in my future job*

Therefore, the second principle to follow in an interview is to show your independence and individuality.

(√) I think / I believe / In my opinion / Personally / As far as I am concerned…

(×) My mother/ my sister /brother told me to do…

Fig. 3.3

(3) Q: *How would your friends and classmates describe you?*

A: *All my friends and classmates like me very much. They like playing and sharing with me. I am rather popular among my friends and classmates.*

This is actually an unadvisable answer because the interviewee does not answer the question in a direct way. To pass the interview, you'd better know the characteristics about both western and Chinese culture.

Western culture can be compared to a Pizza, which presents the main point in a clear way while Chinese culture is much more like dumplings, with details wrapping up the main point (Fig. 3.4).

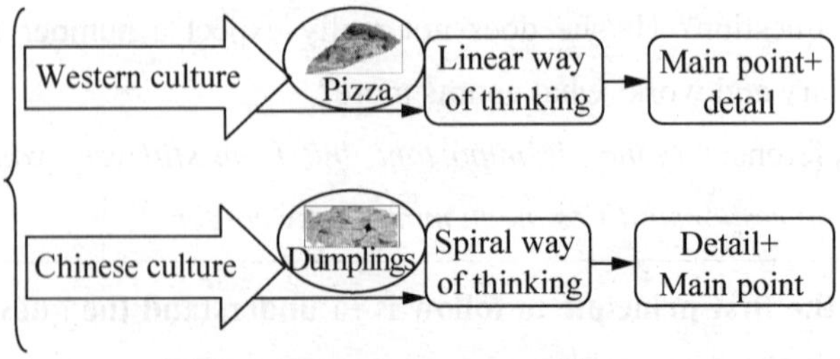

Different ways to answer questions

Fig. 3.4

Answer for reference: *They say I am a kind-hearted and responsible person. When they have some trouble, they all like to turn to me.*

> When you have an English interview, remember to think and answer questions in an English way. **This is the third principle—give a direct answer first and then decide whether or not to make further explanations.**

(4) Q: *If you had one million US dollars to donate, where would you donate it to?*

If your answer is something like "I would like to donate it to the poor", you are talking too generally. An answer with details or examples is much more appreciated than a too general answer, because the interviewer can be better informed with a detailed answer. He/she may get lost in your general talking.

Fig. 3.5

Answer for reference: *If I had such a great amount of money, I would donate it to educational institutions so that poor children can also be educated. Or, I want to donate it to animal conservation institutions to protect rare animals.*

> **Therefore, you should also follow this principle in an interview: answer questions specifically rather than too generally.**

(5) Q: *What does excellent service mean to you?*

A: *For me, excellent service means I should always wear a smile and provide as good service as possible for customers.*

This might be a complete answer or an incomplete one, which depends on the situation. Whether you are supposed to explain why or not depends on the reaction of interviewers. When you finish stating your viewpoint, observe the interviewer's reaction carefully. If he/she waits for your explanation, carry on with your answer. Generally speaking, most interviewers would expect an answer to "why".

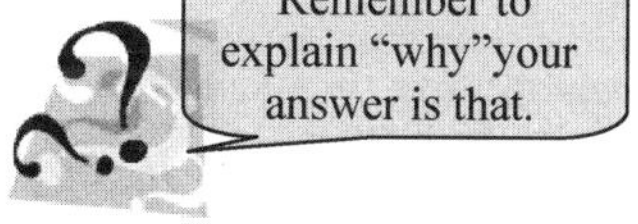

Fig. 3.6

Answer for reference: *For me, excellent service means I should always wear a smile and provide as good service as possible for customers. Because "smile" is the most beautiful language in the world and it can shorten the distance between people. As a hotel employee, serving customers is our vocation. I will wear a smile all the time and try to make customers satisfied when they come to our hotel.*

In conclusion, your answer should be answer plus one, that is, remember to explain "why" your answer is that.

(6) Q1: *What subject do you like least in college?*

Q2: *What is your greatest weakness?*

A1: *The subject I like least is Chinese, because I think it's very boring and we have been learning Chinese for so many years. I don't think it's necessary to spend another year to learn it in College.*

A2: *My greatest weakness is that I am too lazy. (Or I am very careless or I am often late for class...)*

When you confront the first question, do not complain about the so-called tediousness or difficulty of a certain subject. For the second one, never tell your weakness without careful consideration. The above answers are typically wrong, because all they've conveyed to the interviewer is negative, from which the interviewer could conclude that the interviewee may also complain about the perspective job or colleagues or they will definitely not employ you because of your laziness, carelessness or unpunctuality.

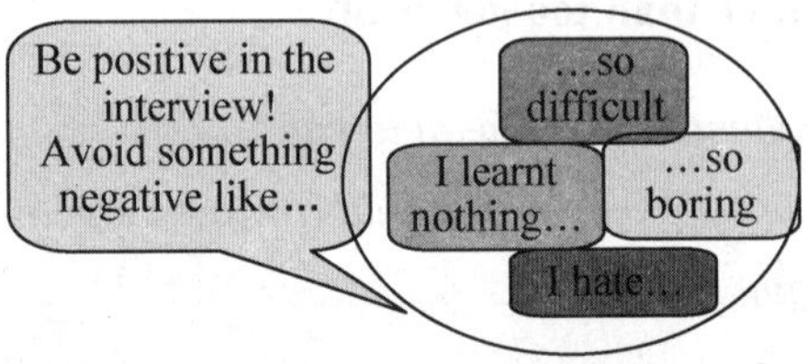

Fig. 3.7

Answer for reference:

A1: *When I just attended college, I was not very interested in Chinese but gradually, I realized every subject exists for a reason and counts. Since then I read many Chinese novels and joined a poetry society.*

A2: *I think my greatest weakness is that I am too careful. Quite often I would check my work very carefully for the second time even though I have finished it as requested. Sometimes this really bothers me and I feel a little bit stressful from myself.*

Remember to be positive during the interview and your positive attitude will help you a lot to get the offer.

(7) Q: *What is your lifelong dream in career?*

A: *I always expect to be a manager in a five-star hotel because hotel management is my major and I like working in hotel industry. I want to devote all my talents and make some achievement finally…*

The above answer lacks a good ending. The interviewee can continue the answer and talk a lot more. The question involved here is how to end the answer properly. There are two ways for reference. One is to repeat the question or viewpoint: that's my opinion or that's my understanding of … The other is to end the answer through your eye contact or other facial expressions including a nod, smile and so on. The last choice is to wait the interviewer to interrupt your answer.

Answer for reference: *I always expect to be a manager in a five-star hotel because hotel management is my major and I like working in hotel industry. That's my lifelong dream.*

How to end your answer…

1. Repeat your viewpoint
2. Tell interviewers through eye contact or other facial expressions

Fig. 3.8

So when you want to end your answer, repeat your viewpoint or drop the interviewer a hint through smile, eye contact, nod and so on.

Moreover, at the very end of interview, remember to express your thanks with a smile and then leave.

Unit 3.4 Analysis of Questions Raised in Different Interviews

Name-brand hotels involved in this textbook are mostly located overseas or in large cities in China, like Beijing or Shanghai, so they would adopt a variety of interviews for the sake of convenience and efficiency, including telephone interviews, video interviews, group interviews and individual interviews etc. In this part, how to prepare for questions raised in different interviews will be analyzed, offering more interview skills for interviewees.

Unit 3.4.1 Interview Procedures

When name-brand hotels announce their recruitment plans, they would receive resumes from many candidates. For human resource department personnel, it is not an easy job to interview all candidates, so the first step before interviews is to select some qualified candidates by screening their resumes. The following presents two English resume templates for reference to help a candidate to make a brief and concise resume to impress HR :

Resume

Personal Information

Family Name:	Given Name:
Date of Birth:	Birth Place:
Gender:	Marital Status:
Telephone Number:	E-mail:

Academic Main Courses

Educational Background

Achievement & Awards

Work Experience

English Skills

Computer Skills

Fig. 3.9

Resume

Personal Information

Family Name

Given Name

Date of Birth:

Major:

Telephone Number:

E-mail:

photo

Educational Background

Work Experience

Scholarships & Awards

Qualifications

Others

Fig. 3.10

After screening resumes, generally speaking, name-brand hotels would interview candidates through telephone or internet (to be specific, on a computer with a camera and a headset), which is called a telephone interview or a video interview. On the one hand, these kinds of interviews could help hotels save employment cost; on the other hand, through telephone or internet, hotels could know more about candidates, including authenticity of their resumes, their background, ability of expression and communication etc. Hotels then could select the most qualified candidates for face-to-face interviews in the next round.

As to face-to-face interview, group interview and individual interview are the most commonly adopted methods. Group interview refers to interview in which a group of 3-10 candidates participate together and candidates may face same questions. In group interviews organized by name-brand hotels, general questions are usually raised and interviewers could select better interviewees by making comparisons, which proves to be an efficient way of recruitment. As indicated by itself, individual interview means one candidate takes the interview exclusively each time, and this is usually when interviewers make their final choices by asking more specific questions related to hotel industry, career development, work experience, positions applied etc.

Unit 3.4.2 How to Answer Questions in Different Interviews

According to the part above, different interviews are endowed with different functions with different questions raised. Based on years of interview records of name -brand hotels (especially hotels stated in Chapter I), questions raised in different interviews can be roughly grouped into three kinds: in telephone interview or video interview questions asked are often based on resumes; in group interview general questions about candidates are usually proposed; questions raised in individual interview are closely related to the job and hotel industry.

1. Telephone interview or video interview

During telephone interview or video interview, interviewers tend to ask questions relevant to the resume, for instance,

(1) It says in your resume that your major is hotel management. Would you please tell me what you've learnt about this major?

(2) How did you get the first-rate scholarship?

(3) What do you think is a good way to learn English?

(4) Can you tell me some of the job responsibilities you do in your spare time?

(5) What's the greatest achievement you've made in college?

...

What's more, interviewees are supposed to be very polite when they pick up phones or hang up. Here are some suggestions: When picking up phones, interviewees could start with such polite greetings as "Hello, Sir/ Madam/ Mr. ***/ Mrs. ***. This is ***speaking." Expressions like "Thank you for (giving) calling me", "Thank you for offering me this opportunity", "Thanks for your time and consideration", "It's really nice talking to you" can be used to end a telephone interview. If it is indeed inconvenient to pick up phone calls, interviewees can make explanations, for instance, "Thank you for calling me, Mr. ***. But it is too noisy now and I couldn't hear you clearly. Would you mind leaving your phone number and I will call you back a moment later?"

2. Group interview

Interviewers mainly ask general questions in group interview, which make it much more like chatting. For example:

(1) Could you introduce yourself in English?

① Your English name is …? Why do you choose this name?

② How old are you?

③ Who's this in this picture? What's the relationship between you and him?

(Students prepare some pictures and interviewers raise questions about them.)

(2) Why do you want to work abroad?

(3) Why do you want to work for our hotel?

(4) What is your advantage or disadvantage?

(5) Can you use three words to describe yourself?

(6) How do your friends / colleagues describe you?

(7) What are your hobbies? /What do you often do in your spare time?

(8) Who is your English teacher? Try to describe him/her.

(9) What is the great achievement you've made?

...

In this part, expressive and communicative abilities rank as the top two most important skills to be tested, so interviewees should invest much time and efforts cultivating their interpersonal communicative potentials.

3. Individual interview

Questions ranging from hotel industry, hotel management, positions in the hotel to interviewees' work experience, professional knowledge, and career development could be covered in individual interview. Typical questions are as follows:

(1) Which position do you want to apply for?

(2) Why do you want to work as a waitress/room attendant/cashier/commis?

① Working as a waitress/room attendant/cashier/commis is a tiring job. Can you manage to do it?

② You worked as a doorman. Why do you want to apply for room attendant now?

(3) What do you think is the best management?

(4) What do you think is important in this job?

...

Interviewers aim to test the professional qualifications, expertise and personal potentials of interviewees. Consequently interviewees are supposed to improve professional accomplishment long before the individual interview by attending classes in college, learning by themselves, doing internships in hotels, making career plans etc.

Conclusion

Getting the offer is when full preparation meets good opportunity. Full preparation refers to your knowing yourself and the position, with conviction that you really want the job and the job suits you indeed. Opportunity is the interview itself. In this chapter, the variety of questions, interviewer's motives and principles to follow in an interview are analyzed, all of which can be included into interview skills. With these skills, hopefully you can have a successful interview and get the offer.

Exercise

The following is a group simulation interview. The interviewer is a human resource manager of a five-star hotel in Dubai, UAE (United Arab Emirates), which plans to employ twenty waiters or waitresses and ten room attendants from China. He is interviewing three candidates. One is a sophomore majoring in Tourism English named Angela (A); the other two are Mary (M) and Jenny (J), both majoring in Hotel Management. Read it first and then analyze the answers carefully with what you have learnt in this chapter to see whether they are proper or improper and why. Then do a simulation interview in small groups with your classmates.

Three candidates knock at the door first and go into the room when they hear "come in please" from the interviewer.

Candidates: *Good morning, sir.*

Interviewer: *Good morning. Have a seat please...Now tell me both your Chinese and English names please.*

A: *My name is Li Li. Angela is my English name.*

M: *My Chinese name is Wang Hua. My English name is Mary.*

J: *My Chinese name is Liu Mei. Jenny is my English name.*

Interviewer: *Thank you. Hi, Angela, what position do you apply for?*

A: *I apply for the position of waitress.*

Interviewer: *Why do you want to work in our hotel?*

A: *Because I think Dubai's hotel industry is highly developed and I think working in your hotel can give me the best chance to use what I have learnt.*

Interviewer: *Do you have any work experience?*

A: *Yes, I have. Last summer holiday, I worked as a waitress in a big restaurant for nearly two months. And this work experience made me responsible and trained me into a flexible and sensitive person.*

Interviewer: *Hi, Jenny. How do you understand "sense of service"?*

J: *I'm sorry. I don't understand what you are talking about. Would you please repeat your question?*

Interviewer: *Sense of service.*

J: …?

Interviewer: *Sense of service. How do you understand it with your work experience and knowledge?*

J: *I think keeping a sweet smile is very important. It can make customers warm.*

Interviewer: *Ok. Hi, Mary, what position do you apply for?*

M: *I want to work as a waitress.*

Interviewer: *In F & B?*

M: …?

Interviewer: *Which department do you want to work in?*

M: *I want to work as a waitress.*

Interviewer: *But do you know which department a waitress belongs to?*

M: *I want to work in Food and Beverage Department.*

Interviewer: *Yeah, F & B is short for Food and Beverage Department. Mary, why do you want to go abroad?*

M: *Because I think in Dubai, the hotel industry is developed. It can improve my English. It's a great honor to go abroad. I want to improve myself in your hotel.*

Interviewer: *Jenny, would you like to tell me your purpose of working in UAE?*

J: *Yes. Last year, I joined the National Games of People's Republic of China. During that period, I worked in a four-star hotel as a room attendant for about two months. As a result I really learnt a lot about how to be a qualified room attendant.*

Interviewer: *But what is my question for you? Did you get it?*

J: *About work experience...*

Interviewer: *Angela, could you repeat my question?*

A: *About working in UAE?*

Interviewer: *What's your purpose of working in UAE?*

A: *It can improve my skills and practice myself.*

Interviewer: *In what way?*

A: *Just practice myself in the work process.*

Interviewer: *Ok ... Mary, the same question goes to you.*

M: *I think when I was young, I should try my best to develop for my future. For example, I want to go abroad to improve myself. That's all.*

Interviewer: *Angela, I know that your major is not Hotel Management.*

A: *Yes.*

Interviewer: *But these two candidates have learnt many subjects about hotel management. Compared with you, they have certain advantages. How would you persuade me to hire you rather than they two?*

A: *Thank you for the question. Although I am not a Hotel Management major, I have work experience and know work procedures of waitress to serve the guests. My major is tourism English. I think language is an advantage when I work abroad. And I am a fast learner. On the first day I worked in the restaurant, the manager taught me how to put utensils and serve guests. I did as he told me. He then said, "Good job. You are a fast learner".*

Interviewer: *Good. Hi, Mary, what're your advantages over the other candidates?*

M: *I am sorry.*

Interviewer: *What do you mean? Just tell me your special strong points over others?*

M: *I think my hard-working character deserves recognition, which is regarded as one of my strengths.*

Interviewer: *What about you, Jenny?*

J: *I am not an intelligent person, but I must be a diligent one. As I strongly believe that no pains, no gains. Every one can achieve more than he has done by working hard. Besides, I'd like to make friends with others. I think friends are an essential part of people's life.*

Interviewer: *OK. Angela, in your work experience, have you ever met an angry guest who is hard to deal with?*

A: *Yes. One day, a guest called me and shouted at me, "What's wrong with the fish. It's not fresh." I felt embarrassed because I didn't cook the dish. I knew nothing.*

Interviewer: *What's your response when you heard her shouting?*

A: *I said I was terribly sorry and changed another dish for her.*

Interviewer: *Was the customer satisfied then?*

A: *Yes. She's satisfied with my work.*

Interviewer: *What would you do when your boss is one hundred percent wrong and you know that?*

A: *Sorry, I beg your pardon?*

Interviewer: *Your boss makes a mistake and you know that. He's completely wrong. What would you do?*

A: *I won't tell him directly. I will use my own way to show he's wrong.*

Interviewer: *Mary, what about you?*

M: *I will use my action to tell him.*

Interviewer: *Ok, that's all. Thank you!*

Candidates: *Thank you!*

Interviewer: *Goodbye to you.*

Candidates: *Goodbye.*

Categories of Common Errors & Improper Behaviors in an Interview

Chapter 4

Unit 4.1 Common Errors

1. Pronunciation

As mentioned in Chapter 1, pronunciation is also one of the factors which exert influence on oral communication. Poor pronunciation results in beak-off in communication and makes it difficult to exchange ideas or even causes misunderstanding. Fluent, natural and typical pronunciation enables an interviewee to gain confidence as well as a smooth communication with the interviewers.

In order to improve an interviewee's pronunciation, we need to analyze the errors made in pronunciation.

(1) Confusion of phonemes.

Phonemes	Examples
[i:]→[ei]	see→say he→hey she→shay
[ai]→[e] [æ]	smile→smell like→lack
[e]→[ai]	let→light
[e]→[i]	well→will
[ʒ]→[r]	Pleasure
[θ]→[s]	think→sink thank→sank

(2) Excessively stressed phonemes at the end of a word.

Since there is no voiceless phoneme in Chinese mandarin, Chinese learners of English emphasize the last sound of a word excessively. But in English, there are as many as nine voiceless phonemes such as [p] [t] [k] [f] [s] [θ]. Quite a lot of Chinese learners treat these phonemes as voiced. For example, they tend to say " I helper him to read the booker."

In addition, Chinese people stress too much some voiced consonants and vowels on the end and prolong these phonemes, which also makes the unstressed syllables loud or even louder than the stressed syllables. As the change happens at the end of a word, linking breaks off abruptly and the "loud" sounds hinder the transmission of a word to the following word smoothly and naturally.

As a result, the rhythm and fluency in their speech get lost; and syllables are added to the words and their speech sounds like "Chinglish".

(3) Besides the too stressful sounds at the end of a word, Chinese learners put an emphasis on an unstressed syllable, esp. upon a schwa within a word. For instance, the last tense ending *–ed* should always be a softened syllable when it follows a verb ending with */t/* or */d/*. However, Chinese people would stress it in words like 'visited', 'waited' and 'handed'.

(4) Furthermore, it is worth to be noticed that English native speakers make pauses between meaningful phrases, which makes the speech sound natural and fluent while some English learners do the same between words instead, which puzzles their listeners and arouses troubles and difficulties in comprehension. The sentence "*As a result I really learnt a lot about how to be a qualified room attendant*".

A native speaker would say this way ,

" As a re'sult / I really 'learnt a 'lot/ about 'how to be a 'qualified room attendant."

A Learner would say:

"As a result 'I/'really/'learnt / a 'lot /'about/ 'how/ 'to be a qualified room/ 'attendant".

However, some learners tend to think that the more quickly they speak, the more fluently they are considered to speak. It must be pointed out that haste makes waste. A hasty statement without proper linking, pause, stress or schwa leads to terrible misunderstanding and no communication. And it betrays you as your language is not good enough to catch up with your speech speed.

2. Grammar

In a job interview, grammatical mistakes are made frequently. The following are some typical mistakes with correction and analysis.

(1) 我家并不富裕。

Mistake: My family don't rich.

Correction: My family is not rich.

Analysis: 句中缺少联系动词。

(2) 我家有 4 口人。

Mistake: ① My family has four people.

② There is four people in my family.

Correction: There are four people in my family.

Analysis: ①句不符合习惯；②句的谓语数与主语不符。

(3) 我父母很善良。

Mistake: My parents are very kindly.

Correction: My parents are very kind.

Analysis: 这里需要形容词。kindly 是副词。

(4) 我来到这个学校两年了。

Mistake: I came to the school for 2 years.

Correction: ① I came to the school two years ago.

② I have been in the school for two years.

③ I am a sophomore at the school.

Analysis: 表示一段时间的时间状语 for two years 不和短暂性动词连用。

(5) 老师很负责任。

Mistake: The teachers are responsibility.

Correction: The teachers are responsible.

Analysis: 说明主语的特性要用形容词。

(6) 我是个服务员。

Mistake: ① I am a service.

② I am a servant.

Correction: I am a waitress/ room attendant…

Analysis: ①句不符合逻辑；②句中的 servant 意思为“仆人”，有贬义。不同岗位的服务员有不同的称谓。

(7) 我有好的身体。

Mistake: I have a good health.

Correction: ① I am healthy.

② I am in good health.

Analysis: 不符合英语的表达习惯。

(8) 每周我花 4 个小时学习英语。

Mistake: It will take me four hours to learn English every week.

Correction: ① It takes me four hours to learn English every week.

② I spend four hours learning English every week.

Analysis: 时态不符合。表示现阶段的活动应该用一般现在时。

(9) 我父母很爱我。

Mistake: My parents very love me.

Correction: My parents love me very much.

Analysis: 副词 very 不能直接修饰动词。

(10) 我妈妈是一个家庭妇女。

Mistake: My mother is a housewoman.

Correction: My mother is a housewife.

Analysis:“家庭妇女”没有 housewoman 一说。

(11) 我在餐饮部学会了如何摆台。

Mistake: I learned how to make the table in F&B Dept.

Correction: I learned how to set a table in F& B Dept.

Analysis:“摆台”应译成 set a table.

(12) 我做了客房服务员。

Mistake: I did a room attendant.

Correction: ① I did a job as a room attendant.

② I became a room attendant.

Analysis: 动宾搭配不对。

(13) 我的上司说，我是个好员工。

Mistake: My supervisor says that I am a good staff.

Correction: My supervisor says that I am a good staff member.

Analysis: staff 是一个集合名词，“一个员工”应说成 a staff member。

(14) 尽管我没有什么经验，但是我学东西快。

Mistake: Although I lack experience, but I am a quick learner.

Correction: ① Although I lack experience, I am a quick learner.

② I lack experience, but I am a quick learner.

Analysis: although 是从属连词，but 是并列连词，二者不能同时用。

(15) 我的英语很差。

Mistake: My English is so badly.

Correction: My English is poor/ limited.

Analysis: badly 的词性不对，而且用 poor 比用 bad 更加地道。使用 My English is poor. 显然说话人对自己的英语不自信，而且语气也消极。如果使用“I am still learning English.”则显得比较积极。

Unit 4.2 Improper Behaviors

An interviewer assesses an interviewee all-sided. So an interviewee's aspects such as facial expression, eye contact, appearance and body language are the interviewer's concerns. What should an interviewee do or not do? The following are the do's and don'ts.

1. Do's

(1) Learn about the company you are applying for a job with. In the preparation for an interview, an interviewee may research the hotel and hotel group. There is a plenty of information available online. Try to get the inside scoop on its culture, and use connections that can help you get an interview advantage.

(2) Dress professionally and be groomed appropriately. Your dressing up and grooming reflects your professional quality. The interviewee's image is the first thing an interviewer notices before the former has a chance to speak and shake hands. In order to make a good first impression, you need to dress professionally and separate your social image (if it's more casual, and it probably is) from your professional presence.

Your scent (even if you smell good) can be an issue. An interviewee's favorite perfume or cologne might exert negative impact, which could squash the chance of getting a job offer.

(3) Arrive 10 minutes before the interview starts. Focus your attention to what you have been prepared and the 10 minutes gets you ready psychologically.

(4) Be courteous, respectful and friendly when meeting the interviewer. You might not like the ways the interviewer speaks or behaves, but he is the superior on this occasion. Show your respect to him, which means that you would like to obey supervisors at work even if you have a different opinion.

(5) Make eye contact during the interview. Eye contact is a nonverbal communication. As a Chinese saying goes, "Eyes are the window of heart." Through it, the interviewer will observe the interviewee's internal thought and feeling. It can be too much to attach the importance to eye contact. So make a nonverbal expression that you are interested and self-confident.

(6) Sit still without fidgeting. Walking, standing and sitting in a professional pose and keep your posture till you disappear from the interviewer's sight.

(7) Answer every question and give examples when possible. Obviously "Yes" or "No" is not enough to reply in satisfaction to the interviewer's question. When asked a question, an interviewee should give a definite answer first, followed by necessary concise and specific explanations.

(8) Ask the interviewer to repeat or rephrase the question if you don't understand. It is commonly understandable that sometimes a listener cannot understand the speaker. Even it occurs frequently between native speakers and listeners. So do not cheat yourself that you understand if you miss some key points in your communication. Instead ask politely.

(9) Give complete answers while sticking to the question that is asked. An interviewer can easily find out that his interviewee is not good at the English language when the latter uses too many incomplete sentences, though they are often used in conversations.

(10) Be honest as the interviewer is experienced in discovering lies. " Honesty is the best policy". Even if it lands the interviewee the job, lies are hard to keep up. This dishonesty could come back to bite him and hurt his credibility at the hotel.

(11) Be yourself. Let your personality shine during the interview especially your positive traits. Do not be who you think they expect you to be. If you get the job they will soon find out who you really are.

(12) Show enthusiasm about and interest in the job being offered. Feel excited and stay in high spirits and convey your enthusiasm for the opportunity to interview, along with the solid ability to the job, which will exert a positive influence on the interviewer.

(13) Be positive. You want to show them that you are someone that they would like to work with. To err is human, but you do not have to tell your shortcomings or disadvantages initiatively. Try to take the opportunity of presenting your traits and advantages in such a limited time.

(14) Prepare questions to ask the interviewer to get information you couldn't find

about their organization. Most of the time, the interviewer asks the interviewee questions. However, communication is double-way and mutual and an occasional inquiry would arouse the interviewer's interest as well as show yours.

(15) When the interview is over, leave gracefully. Express your thanks and say goodbye in a friendly way. Close the door gently facing the interview with your heartfelt smile.

2. Don'ts

(1) Don't chew or smell of garlic or smoke. The unpleasant smell would frustrate the people around you and the interviewers as well. And the chewing of gums are annoying on such an occasion.

(2) Don't leave your cell phone on. Don't bring in your cell phone with you. It would be better not bring in your cell phone since any unexpected message or calling would divert your attention from your business. Your 'sorry' to the interviewer is too late, let alone your phone is left behind you, which suggests you are such a person as thoughtless.

(3) Don't be extreme in your posture. Don't slouch, don't lean back, and don't sit stiffly on the edge of the chair. Your slouch, leaning back and stiff posture indicate your lack of interest in the job, nervousness and laziness, which affects you negatively as an employee in hotel service industry.

(4) Don't say negative things about others or a previous job. Any complaint about the people you dealt with or the job you did in the past would impress the interviewer that you are not so cooperative as he expected.

(5) Don't say "I'm nervous." In fact, proper nervousness helps you to focus your attention on your task. Everyone will feel more or less nervous on your feet. But being too nervous would pose a negative influence on your performance. Even if you say you are nervous, you won't be apologized. On the contrary, the interviewer would suppose that you aren't self-confident enough.

(6) Don't lie. The interviewer is alert at your lies. You have to tell another lie to cover the former one, which forces you into an embarrassing situation. Once he sees through your lies, the result would be serious.

(7) Don't say you want to work at the hotel for the purpose of improving your English and then come back to China. The boss employs you and pays you the salary in order that you will work for him rather than learn English at the hotel. And when you start working at the hotel, you will not be so skillful. After years of work, you get more and more qualified. In this case, he wishes you will work for him for a longer time.

(8) Don't appear to be only interested in the salary. Salary is important undoubtedly,

but it can't be put on the top priority, esp. for a youth who is supposed to develop his own professional skills and abilities first of all. It is wise not to mention it till the interviewer brings it up.

(9) Don't say that the job you're applying for is "hard" or "difficult". It seems that you are not confident about dealing with tough situation or overcoming obstacles at work. 'Challenging' is a word to replace 'hard' or difficult' in a positive way. And you'd better assure the interviewer that you are ready to face the challenge.

(10) Don't leave or get up to leave in the middle of a sentence. Do not take your steps and leave till you say good-bye to the interviewer. If you do not finish your last words before you leave, it seems that you want to escape the spot as soon as possible, which indicates that you are not mature enough.

Questions:

(1) What are your disadvantages? What do you think you can do to improve yourself?

(2) Do you believe that some slightest errors can betray yourself?

Standard standing posture (√)

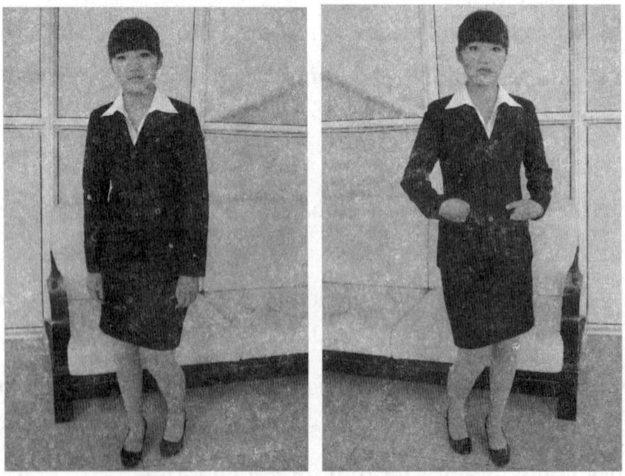

Nonstandard standing posture(×)

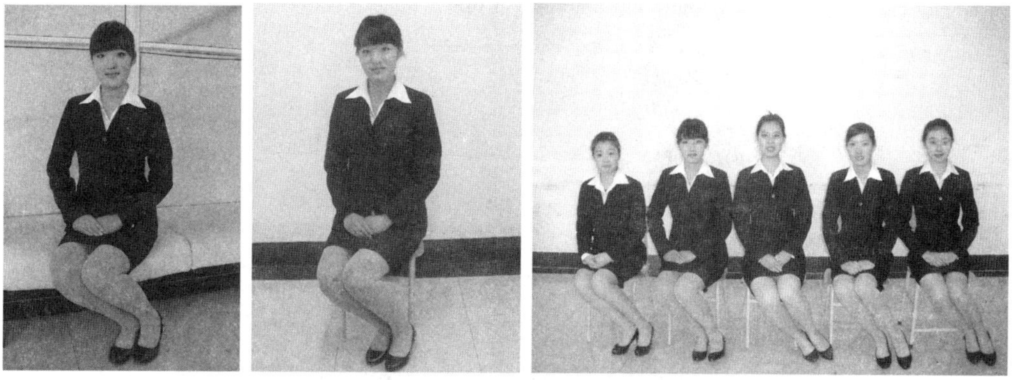

Standard sitting posture (√)

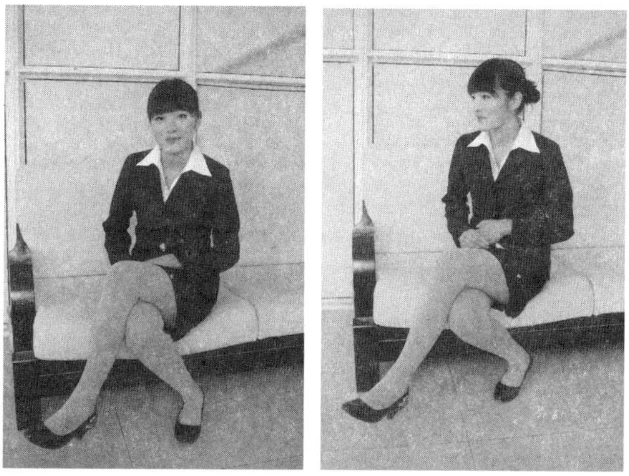

Nonstandard sitting posture(×)

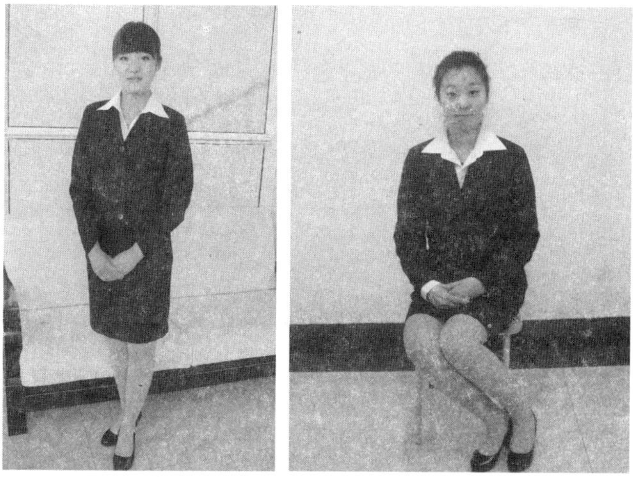

Formal dressing(√)

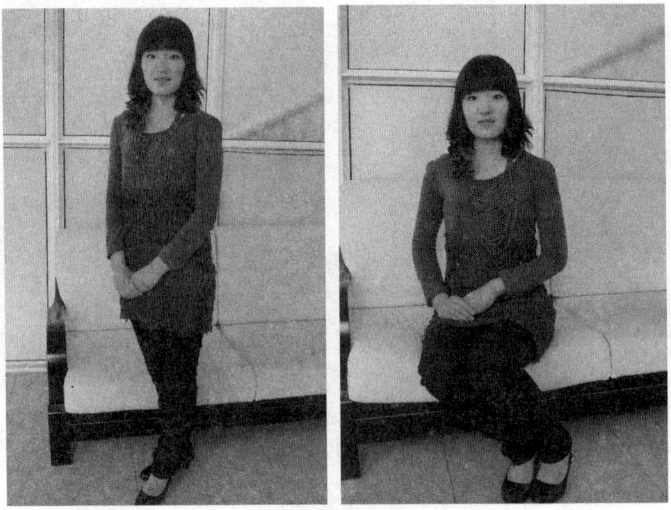

Informal dressing(×)

Introduction to Different Departments in the Hotel and Corresponding Duties

Chapter 5

Unit 5.1 Departments in the Hotel

The Front Office

The Front Office is the part of the Room Division Department. Director of the Front Office runs the department. This department ensures that the customers are treated well in every regard. For example: the taking of reservations, picking guests up from the airport, bringing them to the hotel, checking them in, checking guests out, the operation of hotel facilities etc. Most of the employees in this department work at the front of the house, which means that they should be very well-mannered, honest, warm-hearted, polite, responsible, patient, smart, efficient, and alert. Employees who work in the back of the house should have the same personality and manners as well. The only difference between the front of the house and back of the house is whether you are facing guest directly or indirectly. The Front Office Department has its sub-divisions, which look after each and every place individually but ultimately report to the Director. The below-mentioned sub-divisions are found in most internationally recognized hotels. We may find some difference from one hotel to another.

1. Reservations

The main work of this department is to take the customer's reservations. Some hotels only take room reservations but others also take reservations for the food and beverage outlets. It means that the people who work in this department should have very good command of English. Their voices should be natural, clear and their manner polite. They should also be patient, concerned and active, with smile on their face all the time. The staff should take the initiative to learn more about the hotel facilities, prices and other general information.

2. Reception

One of the most important places in terms of the overall impression made on the guest is the Reception Department. The main objective of this department is to deliver efficient check-in and checkout services to the guest in accordance with the standards of the hotel. The key role of this department is to inform the other related departments about guest choices, orders and information. The most important and difficult job in reception is to gather data and keep records of each guest who checks into your hotel. The main object of the hotel is to serve as a "Home away from Home". If we are not aware of our guests and their preferences it is almost impossible to deliver personalized service. That is why keeping guest records is very important. Reception is responsible of that. This department also deals with money, which means that people who work in this department must be very honest, conscientious, and flexible. In order to provide quick and effective service, file management and time management training is very important and necessary for employees of this department. People who work in this department are called Receptionists or Guest Service Agents. Some hotels may offer traditional welcomes to guests such as Chinese, Arabic, Nepalese, and American etc. Guest Service Agents are also responsible for welcoming the guests according to local customs.

3. Concierge (Bell Boy)

This department is also one of the most important departments in the hotel. This department is responsible for delivering the guest's luggage. To work in this department you must be honest, hardworking and flexible. While transferring the luggage, you need to inform the guest about the hotel's general information, on-going promotions in different outlets at the hotel, general information about the city including place of interest. This department is also responsible for different guest amenities such as: magazines and newspaper delivery, ticket booking, booking of city tours, delivery of faxes, mail, documents etc. Employees in this department should also take the initiative to know something about the guest who is checking in and checking out so that they can provide proper service in as efficient a way as possible. In some hotels, Valet Service, which means car parking service, also falls under the control of this department.

4. Operator

This is a very small department within the Front Office Department. However, it is very important in the day to day operation of the hotel. Reservations deal with the reservation process, but the operators are in charge of incoming and outgoing calls. They are also in charge of redirecting telephone calls from one department to another. Smiling is the most important factor in Hospitality Industry. People cannot see you when you answer the phone but they can feel how you are saying something. That is why posture and body language while talking on the phone leaves an impression on the guest. That means you have to be very careful and polite while working as a Telephone Operator. Some of the operator's responsibilities are: answering phones, sharing information, answering a guest's questions or following up on unanswered questions and providing them with the answers later on, redirecting in-house telephone calls etc. The most important thing to remember as a telephone operator is not to share any confidential and private information about the hotel and the guest.

5. Butler Service

This department also comes under Front Office Department. Most of the hotels do not have this department. However, high-end or luxury hotels may offer this service to guests. The main objective of this department is to provide excellent, personalized, and customer focused service to the guest. A person who works in this department is also called an ambassador of the hotel and represents the height of the luxury. When we talk about personalized service, it means that the individual guest will be served by the individual staff members at all times and on all occasions. The Butler is fully responsible for fulfilling each and every of the guest's requests. This department will also organize small in-suite celebrations for the guest to give them the family touch or personalized service. Employees of this department should have basic knowledge about both the Housekeeping and Food and Beverage Departments. Some of the most important responsibilities of this department are: Packing and Unpacking service, In-suite amenities, Bath Menu, Pillow Menu, Birthday Celebration, Anniversary Celebration, Service of Light Meal to Heavy Meal, Tea and Coffee

Service etc. This department is also responsible for maintaining the guest history book by updating the information. i.e., the guest's routines and schedules, and what the guest expects from the hotel. In this way the butler delivers all the necessary services in accordance with the hotel's standards and procedures at the right time and right place to the right person.

6. Business Center

This outlet is run under the guidance of Front Office Department. As the name suggests, this outlet takes care the business needs of the guest. Hotels that mostly target business travelers as their main customer may have bigger space for this department. Business travelers who need to do some office work while staying in the hotel may be able to get help from this department. The main objective of this department is to provide office help for the customer. For example Internet service, photocopying, fax service, typing service etc. Some hotels may offer light food and some specialty beverages in this outlet as well. Employees of this department must have good knowledge about computers, as well as basic knowledge about Food and Beverage Service.

Answer these questions.

(1) What are the different sections in the Front Office Department?

(2) Why is butler service important for the hotel?

(3) What are some qualities you should have to work in Front Office Department?

(4) What are the responsibilities of Bell Boy?

Housekeeping

Housekeeping is the most important department in the hotel under the Room Division. Housekeeping is a combination of two words: House + keeping. This means to keep the house clean, neat, and tidy in accordance with the standards of the hotel. These are very important and basic aspects of Housekeeping but they also need to help create an environment that makes the guest feel at home. The main objective of this department is to provide a clean and comfortable environment for the guest and the hotel's employees. A clean environment is very important to everyone. It can affect people's mood in a positive way. The Housekeeping department is one of the largest of a hotel's departments. It also has more employees than any other department. This department also helps to organize banquets, exhibitions, conventions, conferences and in-suite celebrations. In fact, the objectives of the Housekeeping Department are numerous. Let's talk about these objectives individually, which will make them easier to understand. Coordination of the different work areas and job responsibilities, cooperation between employees and teamwork between them are the hallmark of a good and successful housekeeping department.

Room attendants are responsible for cleaning the rooms, refilling the mini-bar, providing extra in-room items for the guest, providing daily useful necessities, maintaining the cleanliness of the hotel corridors, provide turn down service, offering other services to the guest as per the hotel policy etc. Public Area Attendants are responsible for cleaning the public areas. Public areas are all of the places in the hotel where guests are allowed to walk around or visit. They are also responsible for cleaning the service corridors, outlets and offices in the hotel. The Linen room is in charge of receiving the soiled linen and distributing fresh linen as per the request of each department, including housekeeping. They are also responsible for maintaining stocks and keep records of every thing. Laundry is responsible for cleaning the linen used by individual outlets, hotel rooms as well as guest's clothing. They are also responsible for delivering guest's clothing to their rooms or butler. The Housekeeping Department is also responsible for delivering flowers and plants for different functions organized by different outlets or departments. It is also responsible for the flowers and plants, delivery of special flower bouquets to the customers on request. Some luxury hotels may offer free flower bouquet services for guests on special occasions. This section of housekeeping department is also responsible for maintaining the gardens around the hotel or within the hotel.

As you can see, many individual departments within housekeeping department are responsible for different sections so that they can achieve their targets and goals. The head of the department is called The Executive Housekeeper. They are responsible for planning, implementing, budgeting and reporting to their seniors for the whole department. As all of you know this department is extensive, the work areas are large, and the responsibilities of the department are many. That is why in some hotels this department may also include the position of Housekeeping Coordinator whose main responsibility is to share information between all the different sections and different departments. They must make reports, divide the responsibilities between different employees, update data, maintain cost control and work as a telephone operator for the housekeeping department.

Answer these questions.

(1) Describe the responsibility of housekeeping attendants in brief.

(2) Why is housekeeping department very important in hotel?

(3) What do you understand by "Public Area Attendant"?

Food & Beverage Division

Another of the most important departments in a hotel is Food & Beverage division. In this division, other subdivisions have separate work areas and responsibilities. In this lesson, we will learn about those subdivisions individually. The Food and Beverage Division looks after everything related to food and beverages. This includes:

(1) Placing purchase orders.

(2) Receiving goods from the purchasing department.

(3) Preparing the goods for sale and consumption.

(4) Serving them according to standard service procedures.

(5) Maintaining a hospitable environment at all the outlets.

(6) Doing the accounting for individual outlets or departments.

(7) Providing training for departmental employees to maintain the service standards established by the hotel.

(8) Responsibility for food safety and hygiene, etc.

The head of this division is the Director of Food & Beverage or Executive Manager for Food & Beverage. The subdivisions are as follows.

1. Food & Beverage Service

This is one of the most interesting and challenging departments in the hotel. Some hotels may call this department only Food & Beverage Department. However, this department also looks after the service part of food and beverage. Since the beginning of the hotel industry, this department has been the main generator of profit as well as the most important in terms of the impression the guest leaves with. Service department standards may vary in every hotel, but the basic rules apply to every hotel, no matter the size. The F&B Manager, whose job includes implementing the hotel's standards, budgeting, planning and reporting to his or her superiors, runs this department. Some of the important work undertaken by this department includes:

(1) Checking the market value of various goods.

(2) Obtaining high quality goods and insuring their proper preparation in conjunction with the kitchen staff.

(3) Setting the standards for how to serve different food and drinks.

(4) Preparing the menus and pricing for each and every outlet.

(5) Training the staff.

(6) Setting the target for every outlet.

(7) Coordinating with sales and marketing staff.

(8) Surveying the market from time to time; and updating the items as per the needs and demands of the guests.

Many hotels may have different F&B outlets, but most of the high star hotel offer 24 hour Room Service, a Fine Dinning Restaurant, Signature Restaurant, Casual Restaurant, Coffee Shop, Lounge Bar, Night Club, Specialty Restaurant, Local Cuisine Restaurant, and Pool Bar or restaurant. This department really depends on the Kitchen Department.

2. Reservations

Another most important sub-division of F&B is Reservations. This department takes care of reservations for all of the outlets of the hotel. The success of the restaurant really depends on how well the reservations department handles customer calls and whether or not they can convince guests to come to your hotel restaurant and dine with you. The most important thing to remember while working as an reservationists is to follow up on the bookings for every outlet remaining aware of how many guests have made reservations and how many more can be accommodated. It is very important to mention every guest request on the reservation sheet with comments and to follow up with the manager or appropriate person within the outlets in question. Working in this department you must have every detail written down on the paper and follow up on your preliminary work. Filing and basic knowledge of computers and telephone etiquette is very essential. People who work in this department should know all of the relevant information from every outlet, i.e. any ongoing promotions, basic menu knowledge and pricing, capacity of each outlet etc.

3. Kitchen

The Kitchen is where the food to be served is prepared. In any kitchen, good hygienic conditions are an absolute necessity. A modern kitchen must be equipped with all of the necessary things to safely prepare, present and store food. This includes a stove, an oven, a microwave oven, a sink with running water to clean ingredients before preparation and wash hands, as well as an automatic dishwasher. The quality of food and speed of service depend on efficiency, hence planning, kitchen design and layout must be undertaken with due care and expert advice if necessary. Errors committed in planning of purchasing equipment for a kitchen are extremely costly in the end. A poorly planned kitchen results in high costs, slow production, unhappy kitchen staff, and dissatisfied guests. Ideally, kitchens should be planned according to the menu envisaged. This will allow proper equipment selection, layout, determination of production capacity and appropriate purchasing. Today's high rents and construction costs dictate wise use of every square inch of space. Restaurateurs and other people concerned should be knowledgeable about both cooking and space allocation. The most qualified people in kitchen planning are experienced and successful chefs. They know from experience the best and most efficient equipment, layout and spacing. A good and ideal kitchen should have the following features.

(1) Lighting: Every kitchen must be well illuminated to prevent accidents, increase efficiency, facilitate quality control and prevent waste. Fluorescent light fixtures are advisable for their efficiency and cool operating temperatures.

(2) Ventilation: Ventilation is of great importance in any kitchen. It prevents odors from penetrating the dining area and increases the well being of cooks. This in turn improves quality and efficiency. Some operators actually air condition their kitchen with laudable results.

(3) Sprinkler Systems: All kitchens and restaurants must have an appropriate sprinkler system. This is essential in case there is a fire.

(4) Floor Coverings: Kitchen floors must be non-slip to prevent accidents. If tiles are used, cover them with a non-slip coating. Continuous non-slip floor covering containing stone chips is the most suitable. It can be applied quickly and inexpensively. They are easy to clean and prevent insect infestation.

(5) Wall Coverings: Kitchen walls can be covered with tiles or durable high gloss finish paint. Tiles are initially expensive, but are durable and easy to clean. High gloss finish paint is more expensive in the long run and less sanitary.

(6) Kitchen Equipment: Kitchen equipment can be conveniently grouped into five categories: storage, preparation, cooking, accessories and service equipment.

(7) Storage Equipment: It consists of industrial food-grade shelving. It may be wire or solid. Wire shelving is appropriate for canned goods or boxes; solid shelving is required in refrigerators and freezers. It is easy to clean. All shelving must be arranged appropriately to facilitate adequate air circulation.

(8) Preparation Equipment: This consists of all equipment employed in food preparation (chopping, dicing, cubing, peeling, slicing, mixing, processing). It speeds up all of these tasks, reduces labor facilitates quality control and promotes consistency.

(9) Cooking Equipment: All equipment used in cooking falls under this category and may be fuelled by electricity, propane, natural gas, oil, wood or steam. The fuel must be selected with due care according to availability and style of cooking being envisaged. Steam generators are available as is cooking equipment with self-steam generating installations.

With all of these features in a kitchen, everything will be in order and chances are everyone involved will be satisfied with the result.

4. Stewarding

Another most important department in F&B Division is the Stewarding Department. Stewarding is the backbone of the food and beverage department. The main responsibility of this department is to clean the dishes and assist Kitchen Department to maintain hygiene for food safety. As it is necessary to provide quality service and food to the customer, the Stewarding Department is of vital importance. Inventory of Operating Equipment is another of this department's important jobs. This department takes inventory for all the F&B operating equipment such as crockery, cutlery, flatware, stemware, silverware and buffet decorative pieces. The staff from this department writes breakage reports for every outlet, maintaining an efficient work place and operational equipment so that the staff can perform quickly and maintain a high level of work standards. The Stewarding Department helps the kitchens and Food and Beverage Department to maintain a clean workplace, hygiene and safety to ensure that satisfactory service is provided to the customer. The staff of this department is most important and valuable to the hotel. That is why people often say, "They (the staff) are the unsung heroes".

Answer these questions.

(1) What does Food and Beverage Service Department do?

(2) What makes good kitchen?

(3) Why is stewarding important in hotel?

(4) Name different food and beverage outlets in the hotel.

Recreation

The Recreation Department is one of the most important departments in ensuring the guest's relaxation. This department offers the most advanced and professional fitness facilities to the guest. The facilities may include a fully equipped gymnasium, swimming pool, squash courts, sauna and steam rooms as well as Jacuzzis. Some hotels may offer an aerobic studio for fitness classes as well. A Spa and massage center is also a quite common outlet that guests can find in every standard 4 or 5 star hotel. They employ dedicated and highly skilled therapists and masseurs who are experts in the arts or relaxation, rejuvenation and pampering. Some hotel may offer water sports for their guests as well such as waterskiing, kayaking, boat trips etc. As part of the Recreation Department some hotels may have retail shops to their guests, where guests can find some signature, valuable gifts for their family and friends.

Sales & Marketing

Today's world is modern and competitive. There are numerous hotels in every country. To establish your hotel's brand name and service in the market is the job of the Sales and Marketing Department. The main objectives of this department are achieved through meetings, site inspections, entertainment, and business travel. This department strives to achieve the financial goals set as per the budget. Sales and Marketing maintain and develop a strong relationship with different guests. Sales and Marketing also initiates strong and innovative partnerships with the market to enhance the brand and positioning worldwide. Many types of guest choose to stay at any given hotel. Rack/Fit means individual guests who book directly by themselves. Leisure guest means those guests who booked the hotel by Travel Agents or Tour Operators. Corporate guest means those guests whose company booked the hotel for the guest. Groups guest are those guests who have booked multiple rooms and use other hotel facilities for there own program such as meetings, conferences and other events. Sales and Marketing also promote conference and banqueting facilities to the guest.

Finance

The main purpose of every business is to make money. The hotel industry sells services through the staff to make sure that the value of guest's money for the guest is maximized by exceeding their expectations. The finance department deals with the hotel's money matters. This department is very important in the hotel. The main goal of the Finance is to provide the best levels of performance and support for the business and the individual through simple creative solutions. Finance keeps records of the hotel's income and expenditures. The department then uses this data to calculate the net profit each month. A good finance department should excel at this function.

1. Finance Management

The Director of Finance, the Financial Controller and the Finance Manager deal with day to day running/managing of the accounts office, Financial reporting/planning and general analysis of performance of the hotel Balance Sheet and reviews.

2. Income Audit/ Night Audit

Ensure that all income is received correctly, systems are reconciled and that correct procedures are followed.

3. General Cashier

The cashier deals with all cash intake and floats of all the staff.

4. Accounts Receivable

Approves credit for all non-cash paying guests, sends out all the customer bills, follows up and on customer queries and follows up on obtaining payment.

5. Accounts Payable

Deals with all invoices and pays them, ensuring that invoices are approved and account coding is correct, etc.

6. Payroll

Payroll handles all payroll issues. This department is also responsible for paying salaries, overtime, allowances, service charge, etc.

7. F&B Control

F& B Control monitors and reports on all Food and Beverage costs and sales; maintains control over discounts and stocks; Analyzes specific areas of the operation to determine profitability and to aid in decisions to change services or products offered.

8. Stores

Ensure sufficient levels of stocks and stock rotation, and issue all store goods to the department.

9. Receiving

Checks quantity and quality of incoming goods, distributes all items to the relevant departments.

Answer these questions.

(1) What does recreation mean in hotel?

(2) Why is sales and marketing important?

(3) Describe finance roll in the hotel.

(4) What does night audit mean?

Technical Services (Engineering)

Another highly important hotel department is Technical Services. This department takes care of the maintenance work for the entire hotel. The subdivisions of this department may vary from one hotel to another, but there are generally two sections in this department. The first is called Front of House. The Front of House team is responsible for the maintenance of all the areas with which the guests come into contact. This section can be broken down as follows: Room Care, Public Area Care, Electrical, AC, Plumbing, Pool, Carpentry, Masonry, Painting and Upholstery. The Back of House team is responsible for the maintenance of all the areas with which the guest has no contact. This section includes the following: Electrical, AC, Plumbing, Mechanical, Kitchen, Carpentry, Painting etc. If a hotel has an aquarium and special features such as Internal and External Water Features, Fire Features, Internal and External Show Lighting or Façade Projectors, maintenance and upkeep of these things also comes under Technical Department.

Security

Safety and security is one of the utmost concerns these days around the world. The security of the hotel, its guests and staff are the responsibility of this department. The different sections within the Security Department are as follows.

1. Entrance Security

Each employee must pass through Entrance Security upon entering and exiting the hotel. They may not remove any hotel property from the premises unless authorized by the Department Head. Entrance Security is also responsible for keeping records of the every employee's daily arrival at and departure from the hotel. They also keep records of every visitor to the hotel and issue them visiting cards to allow them the required level of access to the facilities or employees. They also keep an eye on every guest who comes to the hotel and keep records of their vehicles.

2. Room Security

This section is responsible for taking care of the entire hotel. They make rounds from time to time to ensure that the hotel is safe and secure. Modern technology had many jobs easier and work places safer. For example sensors and security cameras installed in the hotels make security work easier. The cameras in the entire hotel enable the security staff to monitor them.

Every member of the hotel is responsible to make work place safer and comfortable. If there is any doubt about anything, every member of the hotel should report to the Security Department as soon as possible. So that they can take action in advance or keep eye on doubtful things to prevent accident or unusual things.

Information Technology Department (IT)

One of the more recent additions to the family of hotel departments is the IT Department. As the world has become more modernized and computerized, this outlet has taken on an important role at the hotel. Any problems involving hotel computer systems or different guest requests are taken care by this department. The work done by this department includes:

(1) 24 hours support for the hotel's software systems such as Fidelio, Micros, or Epicure.

(2) The IT department also assists the guests special requests for laptop connections, Internet connections, peripheral devices (memory sticks, memory cards, digital cameras, web cams, etc.), fax machine support.

(3) This department also handles requests or problems any other computer related.

Television is the most common form of entertainment for many people staying in hotels. Many hotels offer many national and international TV channels for their guests, a responsibility which also falls under the domain of the IT Department. They provide TV channels by special requests to the guests for a fee or free of charge depending on the hotel's arrangements. Some hotel IT Departments are also responsible for the design of the hotel's web page and update it regularly.

Answer these questions.

(1) What does engineering department do in hotel?

(2) What is the difference between Entrance and Room Security?

(3) Name some of the responsibilities of IT Department?

(4) Why is security important in hotel?

Human Resources

This department is responsible for the company's single most important asset, its employees. This department ensures that each and every employee is treated fairly. They apply the same rules and regulation to local or international employees. The Human Resources Department always maintains the human factor in all business related decisions. Here are some of the responsibilities of the Human Resources Department.

1. Welfare

This department takes care of all the staff's wellbeing and happiness which are assessed through different standards and procedures established by the hotel. It also carries out safety measures and high leaving quality for the staff.

2. Compensation and Benefits

Another major task undertaken by the Human Resource Department is to finalize compensation and benefits for the employees. If the quality of an employee's does not satisfactorily meet the hotel's standards then company may dismiss said employee. In that case HR Department may pay compensation to this employee in accordance with local rules and regulations. HR is also responsible for giving certain benefits like medical, food and accommodation, transportation, uniforms as per the rules and regulations of the hotel.

3. Communication and Recognition

HR is the department where the staff can go to get help or resolve any problems they may have at work or with the accommodations provided by the company. Some hotels may have different schemes whereby employees can make suggestions, lodge complaints, such as an open door policy, a consultative committee, a discussion program, or allow them to speak directly to the Manager. Every hard working and effective staff member should be praised and recognized, which is why many hotels offer Employee of the Month, Employee of the Year or Employee of the Quarter awards in recognition of outstanding service.

4. Social Gatherings

Everybody needs some sort of social life. If you work aboard some hotels may organize some special social gatherings for the foreign staff such as Christmas parties, annual staff parties, on New Year's Eve, National Day etc. All of these gatherings take place in the hotel or at the accommodations, are managed by HR Department.

5. Performance Management

The HR department is also responsible for keeping track of the employee performance reports. Every hotel may have a different way of assessing the performance of the staff. Here are some examples: The first six months of employment is called the probation period. Every week new employees have to do some work related to training for the outlet to which they have been assigned. The Manager or Team Leader is responsible for conducting that training and reporting to HR every week. Every month the HR department will ask the new employees to report to the department and discuss their progress with the HR Manager. After six months, the outlet manager will make an appraisal of these employees and report to the HR Department. Every year the HR department will make appraisals of all employees to monitor their performance. Some hotels may invite the entire staff to HR on a monthly basis to discuss planning for their future, success at work, benefits and other employee concerns.

6. Recruitment and Selection

HR is in charge of recruiting new employees for the company. Before recruitment, HR will select suitable applicants through interviews, consultations with the individual outlets regarding their requirements based on suggestions from department heads. After selection, HR will prepare the employee's contract. A contract is a legally binding agreement between the hotel and the employee that explains the hotel's rules and regulation your duties and responsibilities as an employee, salary and other employee compensation and benefits. After signing the contract, HR will prepare all of the required documents for the new employees and officially hire them for the company.

7. Facilities

HR is in charge of the establishment of new facilities for employees as well as maintaining the old facilities as per the rules and regulation of the company and local government. A happy staff is a productive staff and it is the responsibility of the Human Resources Department to create a comfortable working environment for the hotel's employees.

Training

The most important department for you as an employee of the hotel is the Training Department. This department is responsible for your continuous growth and professional development in work place and in the future. Training and acquiring knowledge is very important for all employees and it is a lifelong process. Some hotel regulations require certain training hours for its employees. Some of the areas covered by the training department are as follows.

(1) New employee induction.

(2) Development programs and training.

(3) Training courses in the hotel.

(4) Training courses at the training center.

(5) Training courses provided by external trainers.

(6) Departmental training.

(7) Recruitment training program.

(8) Management training.

(9) Internships.

(10) Local students.

(11) Training database.

(12) Career counseling.

(13) Cross training.

(14) Budgeting.

Answer these questions.

(1) What does Human Resource Department do?

(2) Name different training programs of the hotel.

(3) Why do staffs need to be happy in the hotel?

(4) Why are trainings important for individual staff?

Unit 5.2 Skills and Abilities for Hotel

Skills and Abilities

1. Skills

Skills are very important to work in the hotel. Skills mean an ability that has been acquired by training. We could basically master our skills by more training or practice. A skill also means the ability to apply knowledge and use them in order to perform better to complete tasks and solve problems. Skills are described as Cognitive (involving the use of logical, creative thinking) or Practical (involving manual dexterity and the use of methods, materials, tools and instruments).

Here are some lists of skills which are essential in hospitality industry.

(1) Speaking: This skill means talking to others to convey information effectively. It is very important in the hotel to convey correct information in understandable tone, polite and

efficient way at every time. Speaking is very important not only to convey message to guests but also to perform well in other aspects and share and convey inter-departmental messages. To have effective team and to show team spirit and great result speaking or communication is very important. Speaking in the hotel must be common and understandable to every staff. Every one must use one language to convey or share their thoughts or ideas.

(2) Active listening: We must at all time listen to others carefully to know what they want and what are there demands or requests. Active listening is another most important skill in the hotel. It means to give full attention to what other people are saying. While you are listening you must take time to understand the points being made. If necessary ask questions as appropriate to make sure that you understand completely. While asking questions you must not interrupt at inappropriate times. You have to be focused at all times and make sure that nothing is missed out in conversation.

(3) Service orientation: Service is very important in hotel. At all times we must be active and enthusiastic about helping others or thinking about how to make others satisfy. Service orientation doesn't necessarily mean to serve the customer and make them satisfy; it's the whole working process around you. No matter they are customers, colleagues, or from other departments, we always need to be active and look for ways to help others. This will definitely make work place harmonious and work environment better. When we have better environment we can perform better and achieve goals easily.

(4) Social perceptiveness: In our daily work in hotel we encounter many situations and different people from around the world. We everyday see so many actions, signs and different ways of performing the same thing. In this situation we must be aware of others' reactions and understand why they react as they do. We must be able to understand things easily and quickly on others performance. We must understand others' cultures and ways of doing things and never make fun of or laugh at their ways. As to have a great team we must understand each other and create a better working place to provide better service.

(5) Coordination: It's hard for a single person to achieve or fulfill everything that the guests request at one time. It's even hard for a single person to do each and everything without making a plan. While working we must skillfully organize the people or things in order to make them work together effectively. We must adjust our actions in relation to others' actions. We must prioritize our work and deal with them one after another to complete the whole task.

(6) Interpersonal skills: The ability to create good relationships between yourself and other people is called interpersonal skills. If you don't have good relationship with others you won't be able to work well and provide excellent service to your customers. Being kind

to others, talking politely, always having smile on face, keeping an eye contact at all times are some important ones.

(7) Emotional intelligence: The ability to recognize and control your emotions to maintain a high level of professionalism with internal staff and external customers is very important. At all times we have to provide excellent service with commitment without being disturbed by your own problems or emotions.

(8) Instructing: In our daily life we have to do lot of things to fulfill our duty. As saying goes "nobody is perfect" we must learn from others or teach others. This skill teaches others how to do something and be better. We must practice everyday and learn to share and teach others. While instructing others we must follow the standards and procedures provided by the hotel at all times.

(9) Active learning: Learning is a life long process. Everyday while we work we need to understand and learn many things. We must try to understand the implications of new information for both current and future problem-solving and decision-making. We must at all time use logic and reasons to identify the strengths and weakness of alternative solutions, for which we must always try to find new solutions, materials or ideas. That's how we can create smooth work environment.

(10) Problem solving: We face lots of problems in our daily work. When we face those problems we must handle them with care and solve them as soon as possible. While solving problems we must think of alternatives and it's consequence. Understanding, communication, knowledge of products, innovativeness, and creativeness are very important while solving problem.

(11) Decision making: Making decision is another important skill in the hotel. While making decision we must consider the best way to transmit our decision. We must have a good communication of channel while letting others know. We must also consider who will be affected by the decision and what likely effect will be on them. We must also anticipate obstacles and objections while making decision. Critical thinking is very important before making decision. We also need to have alternative plans or plan B. If something goes wrong or doesn't work out we should be prepared to formulate or change the decision.

(12) Job task planning and organizing: Each and every member of the hotel staff has their responsibilities. The entire task must be organized and planned before hand. We must follow the standard all the time and complete entire task. We should have knowledge to utilize methods and organization techniques to ensure efficiency and respect others.

(13) Finding information: We do encounter lots of problems and need to find solutions everyday. When we don't have help around we must know how to find the information

ourselves. Being curious and trying to come up with new and better idea in workplace is very important. If we be more enthusiastic and innovative about our work, we could handle situation better and faster. It is so essential to find relevant information to clarify and provide better answer or information to customers or colleagues.

2. Abilities

Abilities are often thought of as innate. Everyone has different abilities and we should find out about them and know how to take advantage of them.

(1) Ability to work under pressure: We must know how to deal with pressure while working. We must develop a working habit where we can deal with it in efficient way. Especially at peak hour where a lot of activities happening around you, you must know how to manage and work in order.

(2) Ability to learn: No one expects you to know it all in the beginning, but we must listen and learn all times. If you don't know, ask questions until you are clear about it. We all learn from mistakes but try to avoid making same mistakes again and again. Always show your concern and try to improve yourself with more knowledge, procedures and rules.

(3) Oral expression and speech clarity: We must talk to people everyday to convey our message or listen to theirs. Oral expression is the ability to communicate information and ideas in speaking so others will understand. We must express ourselves clearly and in understandable language. We must speak slowly, politely and in normal pace so others can understand us. We should always sound natural.

(4) Speech recognition: When we talk to other people we must have an ability to identify and understand the speech of another person at all time. We must know how to appreciate others and gratitude for the suggestions, ideas or thoughts. We should always respect others. opinion and show our acknowledgment to them.

(5) Information ordering: We all have our own way of working or dealing with things. Some people are better at this while others need to pay extra attention to this. The ability to arrange things or actions in certain order or pattern according to specific rule or standard of the hotel is very important to work efficiently and quickly.

(6) Problem sensitivity: While we work we must keep our eye open and pay attention on each and every little things. We must have the ability to tell when something is wrong or is likely to go wrong. If we could have this sense we could avoid lots of trouble in work.

(7) Arm-Hand steadiness and trunk strength: Health is very important to everyone. We must at all time take care of our health and eat healthy. Working in the hotel you must have a good health condition specially trunk strength and arm steadiness. Some people naturally

have strong heath condition where others not. We must eat healthy food and do regular exercise at all times.

Work Styles

There are many styles of work that we carry in hotel. While at work we must understand and respect the aspects of work and follow the standard and complete the task. This doesn't mean how to work in the hotel but it means while we are at work what the things that we should keep in mind are. If we follow this at all time, this will make our work easier. This will teach you how to perform better.

(1) Self control: When we work in the hotel we must maintain our composure. We must at all time keep our emotions and anger in control. At all times we have to avoid aggressive behavior. We must and should control ourselves at all times.

(2) Cooperation: While working we must be pleasant to others and must display cooperative attitude. We must help each other and should know how to take advantage of the situation for shared common goals. We must keep our differences aside for the company's standard procedure and customer's satisfaction.

(3) Social orientation: We can't complete all tasks by working alone. We must prefer to work with others rather than alone. Team work should be given the first priority to everyone. At work we must personally connect with others to create good work environment. We should put our personal ego aside and work for the best outcome.

(4) Integrity: While we work we must be trustworthy and should always act with integrity. We always must be honest and admit our mistakes and avoid telling lies. At all times we must give straight answers to all questions.

(5) Adaptability/Flexibility: We must adapt the change though they are positive or negative. We must be flexible at all times. Every customer and every day is different. We must be open to change. We must consider variety in the workplace and deal with them calmly.

(6) Attention to detail: No matter where you work, which department you work in, back of the house or front of the house, you must be careful about every detail and through in completing the task that is yours. Every small things matter, every job is important, hence every job must be completely done.

(7) Stress tolerance: While we work we get lots of criticism and suggestions, at those movements we must accept them and deal with them calmly and effectively. We should always be patient and positive for every situation.

(8) Independence: You must be independent at work. You should always develop own ways of doing things while following the hotels procedure, standards and consistency. You should not wait for guidance or supervision all the times. You must show your supervisors that you can get things done by yourself and they can trust you with work.

(9) Dependability: While you work people should trust you. They could leave you on your won without any hesitation so that you could fulfill your duties and responsibilities. You must be reliable and responsible for your work. Others can depend on you on fulfilling obligations.

(10) Concern for others: We must show our concern for others. We must be sensitive to other's needs and feelings. We must understand others and be helpful to them at all times. We must create friendly environment and show imitativeness on creating that kind of environment.

Answer these questions.

(1) What is the difference between skills and abilities?

(2) What are your skills and abilities? Explain briefly.

(3) What skills and abilities are important?

(4) How can you control your emotions while working under pressure?

(5) What do we need to keep in mind before decision making and problem solving?

Personal Attributes and Skills

(1) Reliability: People can rely on you. You should respect the time and be punctual.

(2) Commonsense: At all time take logic approach to tasks. Always think before you act and don't be impulsive.

(3) Initiative: Take interest in each and every task. Ask questions if you get stuck. Show your enthusiasm to each task.

(4) Organization and time management: You must be able to plan, prioritize and manage your time.

(5) Honesty: Always be trustworthy, act with integrity. Always answer straight and admit your mistakes and show your willingness to learn from them. Be true to yourself.

(6) Enthusiasm: Always show positive attitude and motivation towards work. Act like you are enjoying yourself.

(7) Commitment: Always take the responsibility of work seriously, focus on your work rather than other stuffs which are bothering you. Show your interest in task you do daily.

(8) Well-groomed appearance: Always present yourself in neat and clean dress up.

Ensure that your hair, nails and shoes are clean. Always practice good hygiene.

(9) Positive self-esteem: Always hold your self confident and have a belief in your worth.

(10) Problem solving: Solve problem swiftly to satisfy your customer and employer. Be cautious while solving and make sure it doesn't happen again.

(11) Communication skills: Communicate clearly with customers, colleagues and employers. Understand other needs and wants and present yourself in understandable way.

(12) Sense of humor: Don't be serious and take things seriously. See the light side of things but don't act like the clown. Always enjoy the task and present yourself with smile.

(13) Adaptability: Be flexible and open to change.

(14) Loyalty: Respect your employer and colleagues at all times. Do not bad mouth anyone and respect confidential things. Do not share confidential things with others.

(15) Ability to work under pressure: Cope with pressure with positive attitude and always be calm and have fun with it.

(16) Customer service: Always attend to the needs and wants of the customers. Always focus on how to exceed their expectations.

(17) Teamwork: Work with the team or lead the team at all times. Work for common goal rather than personal means.

(18) Ability to learn: Listen and learn, ask questions if you have doubts. Learn from your mistakes and try not to repeat them.

(19) Computer skills: Technology plays a bigger role in hospitality. You must have basic computer knowledge and know how to use them for you own benefits.

Answer these questions.

(1) Describe your interpersonal skills.

(2) Which three attributes suit you? Explain.

(3) Describe your personality.

(4) As per your personal point of view, which one is your advantage and which one is your disadvantage. Explain.

Unit 5.3 Duties of Different Positions in the Hotel

1. Receptionist

A Hotel Receptionist job involves dealing with guests on a daily basis. As you work on this field you will check in and check out guests. Take reservations as part of administration work and offering valuable information regarding accommodation and services. Some of their responsibilities are as follows in most of the international chain hotel brands but are not limited.

(1) Prepare useful papers, equipments and forms for daily necessary work.

(2) Maintain reception area and back area.

(3) Meet hotel attendance and grooming standards.

(4) Maintain current Hotel information to be able to provide information to guests.

(5) Receiving and registering guests as they arrive.

(6) Greet the customer and identify his specific reservation.

(7) Register the guest, ensuring that the necessary details are obtained, i.e. name in full, address, whether company or private booking, special rate, VIP, charge details, nationality, passport number, etc.

(8) Allocate room according to reservations list, ensuring that this is what the guest has booked, both in terms of the room itself and the rate to be paid.

(9) Issue the key card.

(10) Fill out necessary form and file it for future references.

(11) Create guest history report as per hotel requirement.

(12) Receive the payment for accommodation.

(13) Liaise or alert concierge so that the guest's luggage is taken to his room.

(14) Keep records in designated place.

(15) Update occupancy list, arrival guest list, in-house guest list.

(16) Be on hand to book and make the call the appropriate time if the client requires to book a wake-up call.

(17) Take care and maintain of all the equipments and asserts.

(18) Maintain knowledge of special programs and events in the hotel in order to recognize and respond to guests needs.

(19) Maintain a high level of product and service knowledge in order to explain and sell services and facilities to guests.

(20) Ensure that all departments, particularly restaurants, are notified of the tariff entitlements.

(21) Receive mails and direct them to the guests in the hotel.

(22) Complete office bulletin book.

(23) Communicate well to ensure effective shift hand-over.

(24) Handle guest requests.

(25) Safe keeping of client valuables.

Keep client valuables safe.

(26) Keep area clean and tidy.

(27) Maintain confidentiality.

(28) Implements department procedures and policies as needed.

(29) Attend to all briefings.

(30) Participate in training.

(31) Demonstrate Awareness of hotel policies and procedures and ensure all procedures are conducted safely and within the guidelines.

(32) Be aware of duty of care and adhere to occupational, health and safety legislation, policies and procedures.

(33) Be familiar with property safety, first aid and fire and emergency procedures and operate equipment safely and sensibly.

(34) Initiate action to correct a hazardous situation and notify supervisors of potential dangers.

(35) Strive for constant improvement and take responsibility for your own performance.

(36) Adhere to Hotel Handbook and general policies and procedures.

(37) Provide information when requested and promotes hotel's services, facilities and special events.

(38) Build and maintain positive relationships with all internal customers and guests in order to anticipate their needs.

(39) Anticipate guest needs, handle guest enquires, and solve problems.

(40) Create a positive hotel image in every interaction with internal and external customers.

(41) Adhere to hotel brand standards.

(42) Demonstrate co-operation and trust with colleagues, supervisors, teams and across departments.

(43) Actively participate in organized meetings.

(44) Interact with department and hotel staff in a professional and positive manner to foster good rapport, promote team spirit and ensure two way communication effective.

(45) Be open to new ideas and make changes in the job and routine as required.

(46) Work in line with business requirements.

(47) Develop/update skills and knowledge (internally or externally) to reflect changed technology or changed work requirements.

(48) Seek feedback on areas of shortfall.

(49) Maximize opportunities for self development.

(50) Ensure that your work quality meets the standards required and complete tasks in a timely and thorough manner with minimum supervision.

(51) Follow standards, policies and procedures.

2. Bell Boy

A bell boy is someone employed in a hotel for the purpose of carrying luggage for the guests as they come or leave the hotel. He should as he welcomes them, go on to show them and escort them to their respective rooms. He may also run errands that may arise in the hotel, during his shift. Their responsibilities will include, but not limited to the following.

(1) Make sure that working area is clean and tidy.

(2) Open the front door for guests (in some hotels).

(3) Meet/greet guests with hotel standards.

(4) Load and unload luggage from the vehicles that the clients either come in with or are leaving in.

(5) Transport baggage to guest room.

(6) Provide valet service on request (in some hotel valet service is an individual department but in some hotel it is provided by bell-boy).

(7) Control standards of service procedures.

(8) Maintain baggage tags.

(9) Delivery newspaper to every room in the morning.

(10) Store bags.

(11) Open room doors.

(12) Give directions on request.

(13) Call taxis if requested.

(14) Assist guests and escort them to locations within the hotel at their request.

(15) Make sure that trollies are always on good condition and available.

(16) Maintain the caddy and its conditions (if required).

(17) Arrange transport to airport or airport pick up.

(18) Report any maintenance job.

(19) To book a wake up call, the bell boy needs to be on hand to book and make the call at the appropriate time (in some hotel wake up call is organized by reception desk or receptionist).

(20) Maintain knowledge of special programs and events in the hotel in order to recognize and respond to guests needs.

(21) Anticipate guest needs, handle guest enquires, and solve problems.

(22) Follow standards, policies and procedures.

(23) Demonstrate awareness of hotel policies and procedures and ensure all procedures are conducted safely and within the guidelines.

(24) Be aware of duty of care and adhere to occupational, health and safety legislation, policies and procedures.

(25) Be familiar with property safety, first aid and fire and emergency procedures and operate equipment safely and sensibly.

(26) Initiate action to correct a hazardous situation and notify supervisors of potential dangers.

(27) Strive for constant improvement and take responsibility for your own performance.

(28) Adhere to Hotel Handbook and general policies and procedures.

(29) Provide information when requested and promote hotel's services, facilities and special events.

(30) Build and maintain positive relationships with all internal customers and guests in order to anticipate their needs.

(31) Create a positive hotel image in every interaction with internal and external customers.

(32) Adhere to hotel brand standards.

(33) Assist guests and escort them to locations within the hotel at their request.

(34) Demonstrate co-operation and trust with colleagues, supervisors, teams and across departments.

(35) Actively participate in organized meetings.

(36) Interact with department and hotel staff in a professional and positive manner to foster good rapport, promote team spirit and ensure two way communication effective.

(37) Be open to new ideas and make changes in the job and routine as required

(38) Work in line with business requirements.

(39) Develop/update skills and knowledge (internally or externally) to reflect changed technology or changed work requirements.

(40) Seek feedback on areas of shortfall.

(41) Maximize opportunities for self development.

(42) Ensure that your work quality meets the standards required and complete tasks in a timely and thorough manner with minimum supervision.

(43) Follow standards, policies and procedures.

(44) Work effectively with customers and colleagues from different viewpoints and cultures.

3. Waiter and Waitress

Food-service workers perform an important job that is always in demand. Waiters at restaurants have a responsibility to serve the customers' needs during the time they are in the restaurant. Their duties and responsibilities will include, but not limited to the following.

(1) Clean agreed designated areas, in accordance with the hotel procedures, morning/evening routines and hygiene requirements.

(2) Change table linen as required and ensure dirty or damaged linen is counted and exchanged for clean, usable items.

(3) Clean and refill cruet and condiment sets.

(4) Ensure that flowers and table decorations are fresh and comply with agreed standards.

(5) Set tables according to the standard, ensuring that all items used are clean, undamaged and in a good state of repair.

(6) Ensure sideboards on stations are adequately stocked with replacement cutlery, linen or other necessary items for service period.

(7) Prepare salads, sandwiches, cheese boards and coffee according to the standards, when this is an agreed duty of the establishment (But in some hotel waiter doesn't have to prepare anything).

(8) Take orders from customers and ensure these are given to the appropriate person (in some hotel waiter doesn't have to take orders).

(9) Inform customers of daily specials, chef specials or any other promotional items.

(10) Anticipate guest needs, handle guest enquires, and solve problems.

(11) Upsell food and beverage products in the department at all times.

(12) Provide information when requested and promote hotel's service, facilities and special events.

(13) Be totally familiar with the composition of all menu items including wines, foods and beverages.

(14) Serve food and beverage in accordance with the hotel standard, but above all in a professional, and courteous manner.

(15) Clean tables and ensure they are cleaned as soon as it is apparent that customers have finished their food or drink with an acceptable balance between speed, yet allowing customers to finish their meal without feeling rushed.

(16) Ensure that customers are correctly charged, present the bill and take payment from the customer, in accordance with the procedures of the establishment.

(17) At all times Be aware of and practise good customer relations, assisting the guest in any way which does not adversely affect other customers.

(18) Attend to customer complaints satisfactorily.

(19) Carry out on-the-job training to ensure subordinate staff can carry out their duties effectively.

(20) Be continually aware of, and maintain, the highest standards of personal hygiene and dress.

(21) Attend meetings and training courses as required.

(22) Demonstrate awareness of hotel policies and procedures and ensure all procedures are conducted safely and within the guidelines.

(23) Be aware of duty of care and adhere to occupational, health and safety legislation, policies and procedures.

(24) Be familiar with property safety, first aid and fire and emergency procedures and operate equipment safely and sensibly.

(25) Initiate action to correct a hazardous situation and notify supervisors of potential dangers.

(26) Strive for constant improvement and take responsibility for your own performance.

(27) Adhere to Hotel Handbook and general policies and procedures.

(28) Build and maintain positive relationships with all internal customers and guests in order to anticipate their needs.

(29) Create a positive hotel image in every interaction with internal and external customers.

(30) Adhere to hotel brand standards.

(31) Assist guests and escort them to locations within the hotel at their request.

(32) Demonstrate co-operation and trust with colleagues, supervisors, teams and across departments.

(33) Interact with department and hotel staff in a professional and positive manner to foster good rapport, promote team spirit and ensure two way communication effective.

(34) Be open to new ideas and make changes in the job and routine as required.

(35) Develop/update skills and knowledge (internally or externally) to reflect changed technology or changed work requirements.

(36) Seek feedback on areas of shortfall.

(37) Maximize opportunities for self development.

(38) Ensure that your work quality meets the standards required and complete tasks in a timely and thorough manner with minimum supervision.

(39) Follow standards, policies and procedures.

(40) Be specific and clear while handing over the shift to others.

(41) Follow opening and closing procedures thoroughly.

(42) Maintain guest log book and staff log book at all times.

4. Butler (Junior)

In some hotel butlers are under F&B management but in some they are under Front Office management. No matter which department they work under they must always cooperate with Housekeeping, Front Office and F&B to fulfill their responsibilities. Their responsibilities will include, but not limited to the following.

(1) Ensure all arrival/expected arrival rooms/suits are checked and in order.

(2) Greet and escort guests to their rooms.

(3) Make sure that pantry and reception desk in your area are clean and well stocked. and prepared at all times according to hotel standards.

(4) Ensure that all the requirements and needs are met and demonstrate a high and consistent level of service at all times.

(5) Ensure that all procedures & responsibilities relating to the Greeting/Arrival procedures are adhered to hotel standard procedures.

(6) Provide quality and personalized services to guests.

(7) Build a thorough rapport with all in-house guests and maintain interaction in order to facilitate guest recognition and obtain specific individual needs, likes, and dislikes in order to maintain guest history files.

(8) Report for duty punctually in accordance to the issued department duty roster.

(9) Provide a full cashier and currency exchange service for guests.

(10) Upsell rooms/suites and cross sell all outlets within the hotel.

(11) Assist and coordinate the arrivals and departures of guests.

(12) Maintain a high level of communication & feedback within the department.

(13) Maintain the privacy and ensures the security of in-house guests.

(14) Handle guests' luggage and other baggage.

(15) Ensure cleanliness of suites for guests.

(16) Manage guests' special requests delivery.

(17) Identify and anticipate of guest needs and immediate action on all of their request

& requirement.

(18) Ensure that all rooms/suites are maintained and serviced as required.

(19) Provide exceptional and memorable services to guests throughout their stay.

(20) Manage guests' garment pressing, shoeshine and other services.

(21) Follow-up and ensure that guests' requests are met in a timely manner.

(22) Complete guests' orders as per the hotel standard.

(23) Coordinate laundry, pressing collection and delivery.

(24) Liaise with other department such as finance, housekeeping, food and beverage etc in order to achieve the guest, expectation.

(25) Attend daily shift briefings.

(26) Taking order for Private Dining (in some hotel which means Room Service).

(27) Deliver and place the Evening amenities or gift.

(28) Unpack/ Pack Guest Luggage as requested.

(29) Provide a full shoeshine service.

(30) Provide Tea, Coffee and Beverage service to all rooms/suites.

(31) Deliver Newspaper and Magazine to all rooms/suites.

(32) Report any suite maintenance requirement according to standard procedures.

(33) Assist and co-ordinate all in room/suite guest needs & requirements.

(34) Refresh the rooms/suites & assist with turndowns.

(35) Ensure a full and complete shift handover.

(36) Maintain full control of Private Bar replenishment, control and ordering of stock.

(37) Continually check all public areas inside and around the designated work area.

(38) Co-ordinate and liaise at all times with the Butler Order Taker/ Butler Team Leader

(39) Perform other duties and responsibilities as required.

(40) Abide by all policies and procedures as laid in the Butler Services SOP Manual.

(41) Adhere at all times to the Butler's Grooming & Uniform Standards.

(42) Abide by all Hotel and Company policies & procedures.

(43) Adhere to all Hotel Health & Safety policies.

5. Commis

The commis chef assists the head chefs in preparing food while building his culinary skills and experience. Commis chefs often cycle through various positions during their tenure in order to help them learn different techniques, meaning that their duties and responsibilities vary. Their responsibilities will include, but not limited to the following.

(1) Produce food of high quality according to standard recipes.

(2) Ensure required mise en place is complete prior to your outlets opening hours.

(3) Ensure all orders are prepared to the correct standard.

(4) Ensure the kitchen is kept clean and tidy and take part in the cleaning schedule.

(5) Check the fridge daily for expired items.

(6) Receive delivery items and make sure they are fresh and as per requested.

(7) Take inventory of the kitchen and order required items.

(8) Carry out any additional tasks and all other duties assigned during the day.

(9) Assist with the preparation, presentation, decoration and storage of the following dishes: Meat dishes/Meat marinades/Carve meats/Fish and shell fish/Sauces for fish and shell fish/Garnishing techniques and methods of service for fish/Buffet Food (preparation and storage).

(10) Communicate politely and display courtesy to guests and internal customers.

(11) Provide direction to the Kitchen helpers, including Cooks, Kitchen Attendants and Stewards.

(12) Communicate to your superior in any difficulties, guest or internal customer comment and other relevant tasks.

(13) Establish and maintain effective employee working relationships.

(14) Attend and participate in daily briefings and other meetings as scheduled.

(15) Attend and participate in training sessions as scheduled.

(16) Prepare in advance food, beverage, material and equipment needed for the service.

(17) Clean and re-set your working area.

(18) Implement the hotel and department regulations, policies and procedures including but not limited to: House Rules and Regulation/Health and Safety/Grooming/ Quality/Hygiene and Cleanliness.

(19) Perform related duties and special projects as assigned.

(20) Demonstrate Awareness of all the policies and procedures and ensure all procedures are conducted safely and within the guidelines.

(21) Be aware of duty of care and adhere to occupational, health and safety legislation, policies and procedures.

(22) Be familiar with property safety, first aid and fire and emergency procedures and operate equipment safely and sensibly.

(23) Initiate action to correct a hazardous situation and notify supervisors of potential dangers.

(24) Log in security incidents and accidents in accordance with hotel requirements.

(25) Coordinate and cooperate with fellow employees and seniors at all times.

(26) Ensure the smooth running of the outlet.

6. Room Attendant

Sometimes referred to as chambermaids or housekeepers, room attendants are responsible for the cleanliness of rooms in hotels, motels and resorts. Their responsibilities will include, but not limited to the following.

(1) Demonstrate and promote a strong commitment to providing the best possible experience for guests and employees.

(2) Clean assigned guest units in accordance with Company standards.

(3) Stock and maintain housekeeping carts and storage rooms.

(4) Report maintenance issues to Rooms Inspector/Manager immediately.

(5) Properly tag lost and found items and turn them in to management.

(6) Perform towel service responsibilities as needed.

(7) Offer guest assistance when needed whenever possible.

(8) Comply with all safety and security policies in accordance with Company standards.

(9) Report daily to the Housekeeping Office in complete uniform, pick up clean rags, section slips and sign at the key control log book for keys to the floors.

(10) Make sure that room attendant's trolley is properly supplied and clean and orderly maintained.

(11) Bring trolley to the designated floor only after through checking.

(12) Clean floor corridors, service areas, backstairs, linen closets and Room Attendants'/ Maids' comfort rooms.

(13) Serve all occupied VIP rooms and guest rooms assigned to him/her according to standard procedures.

(14) Handle guest requests like providing extra beddings or offering a certain kind of food (serving food is in some hotel only).

(15) Clean all checked-out rooms in order of priority specified by Floor Supervisor.

(16) Perform maintenance cleaning in vacant rooms.

(17) Report to Housekeeping Office or Floor Supervisor immediately on any emergencies such as over-flowing toilets, fused light bulbs, etc, and other fixtures or items that may need repair and maintenance.

(18) Report to the Housekeeping Office or Floor Supervisor on any illness or accidents befalling guests, including any other irregularities.

(19) Implement the hotel and department regulations, policies and procedures including

but not limited to: House Rules and Regulation/Health and Safety/Grooming/Quality/ Hygiene and Cleanliness.

(20) Bring immediately to the Housekeeping Office any items that are left behind in check out rooms, making sure that it is properly registered in the Lost and Found log book.

(21) Report any unfinished assigned rooms to the Floor Supervisor for endorsement to the next shift.

(22) Make sure that linen closet and Room Attendants'/Maids' comfort rooms are kept locked when not in use.

(23) Turn in all soiled rags, newspaper and floor keys to the Housekeeping Office before signing out of work.

(24) Ensure that storage area or Pantry area is always maintained and well stocked.

(25) Perform other related jobs that may be assigned.

(26) Take inventory of the minibar to bill guests for anything consumed and restock anything that was taken out (in some hotel this is done by Food and Beverage Department).

(27) Ensure that all appliances and electronics, such as coffee pots, hair dryers, televisions, and heating and cooling elements, are functional.

(28) Take inventory of housekeeping items in the room, reporting anything that is missing or damaged.

(29) Adhere to Hotel Handbook and general policies and procedures.

(30) Provide information when requested and promote hotel's services, facilities and special events.

(31) Build and maintain positive relationships with all internal customers and guests in order to anticipate their needs.

(32) Anticipate guest needs, handle guest enquires, and solve problems.

(33) Provide extra customer service, such as turning down beds, delivering newspapers and picking up dry cleaning or ironing and fulfill requests for extra pillows or towels.

7. Bartender

Their responsibilities will include, but not limited to the following.

(1) Clean agreed designated areas, in accordance with the procedures, routines and hygiene requirements.

(2) Change table linen as required and ensure dirty or damaged linen is counted and exchanged for clean, usable items.

(3) Ensure that flowers and table decorations are fresh and comply with agreed standards.

(4) Set tables according to hotel standards, ensuring that all items used are clean, undamaged and in a good state of repair.

(5) Ensure sideboards on stations are adequately stocked with replacement cutlery, linen or other established needs, be they food or equipment.

(6) Maintain outstanding knowledge of cocktails, beverage and wines.

(7) Display excellent attention to detail and consistency.

(8) Anticipate guest needs & expectations at all times.

(9) Report any guest complaints and suggestions to the Outlet Manager on duty.

(10) Ensure that adequate stocks of beverage are requisitioned on time.

(11) Maintain the mise en place of clean equipment, condiments, tray cloths, cocktail napkins, etc as per the standard operating procedure.

(12) Mix and serve alcoholic and nonalcoholic drinks to the customers of the bar or prepare for the restaurants staff, following standard recipes.

(13) Mix ingredients, such as liquor, soda, water, sugar, and bitters, to prepare cocktails and other drinks as per standards.

(14) Serve beverages to customers and offer snacks or food for them as per availability and procedures.

(15) Order or requisition liquors and supplies from the store.

(16) Make sure all the necessary items in the bar and properly arranged and stocked.

(17) Arranges bottles and glasses to make attractive display.

(18) Arrange, prepare and make slice and pit fruit for garnishing for drinks or cocktails.

(19) Upsell food and beverage items at all times and cross sell other departments or outlets.

(20) Take orders from customers and ensure these are given to the appropriate person.

(21) Inform customers of daily specials, bartender special, chef special, snacks of the day or any other promotion running in the hotel.

(22) Anticipate guest needs, handle guest enquires, and solve problems.

(23) Provide information when requested and promote hotel's services, facilities and special events.

(24) Be totally familiar with the composition of all menu items and how to prepare it.

(25) Serve food and beverages in accordance with the hotel standards, but above all in a professional, courteous manner.

(26) Clean tables and ensure they are cleaned as soon as it is apparent that customers have finished their food or drink with an acceptable balance between speed, yet allowing customers to finish their meal or drinks without feeling rushed.

(27) Ensure that customers are correctly charged, present the bill and take payment from the customer, in accordance with the procedures of the establishment.

(28) At all times be aware of and practise good customer relations, assisting the guest in any way which does not adversely affect other customers.

(29) Be continually aware of, and maintain, the highest standards of personal hygiene and dress.

(30) Attend meetings and training courses as required.

(31) Demonstrate awareness of hotel policies and procedures and ensure all procedures are conducted safely and within the guidelines.

(32) Be aware of duty of care and adhere to occupational, health and safety legislation, policies and procedures.

(33) Be familiar with property safety, first aid and fire and emergency procedures and operate equipment safely and sensibly.

(34) Initiate action to correct a hazardous situation and notify supervisors of potential dangers.

(35) Strive for constant improvement and take responsibility for your own performance.

(36) Build and maintain positive relationships with all internal customers and guests in order to anticipate their needs.

(37) Create a positive hotel image in every interaction with internal and external customers.

(38) Adhere to hotel brand standards.

(39) Assist guests and escort them to locations within the hotel at their request.

(40) Demonstrate co-operation and trust with colleagues, supervisors, teams and across departments.

(41) Interact with department and hotel staff in a professional and positive manner to foster good rapport, promote team spirit and ensure two way communication effective.

(42) Be open to new ideas and make changes in the job and routine as required.

(43) Develop/update skills and knowledge (internally or externally) to reflect changed technology or changed work requirements.

(44) Seek feedback on areas of shortfall.

(45) Maximize opportunities for self development.

(46) Ensure that your work quality meets the standards required and complete tasks in a timely and thorough manner with minimum supervision.

(47) Follow standards, policies and procedures.

(48) Work effectively with customers and colleagues from different viewpoints and cultures.

8. Demi Chef De Partie

Their responsibilities include, but not limited to the following.

(1) Ensure that all stocks are kept under optimum conditions.

(2) Ensure that all mise-en-place is always freshly prepared and on time.

(3) Ensure that all dishes are being prepared to the correct recipe and to the correct quantity.

(4) Assist head chef to plan menu and other necessary items for the kitchen.

(5) Ensure that all dishes reach the hot plate or posses correct garnished, the correct portion and size, presented on the prescribed serving dish in the prescribed manner.

(6) Ensure that his section is being kept clean and tidy at all times.

(7) Ensure that junior cooks and trainees receive the right training and optimum guidance.

(8) Ensure that any anticipated shortages are communicated promptly to the sous chef or head chef.

(9) Ensure that no horseplay is allowed in his section and that all staff under his control are treated fairly and with courtesy.

(10) Deputise in the sous chef's absence and take charge of the kitchen when directed to do so.

(11) Attend training courses and seminars as and when required.

(12) Direst the preparation, seasoning and cooking of salads, soups, fish meats, vegetables, desserts or other foods.

(13) Help head chef on planning and pricing the menu and its items.

(14) Keep records of everything happened in the outlet.

(15) Check the quality of raw and cooked food products to ensure that standards are met.

(16) Monitor sanitation practices to ensure that employees follow standards and regulations.

(17) Check the quantity and quality of received products.

(18) Order or requisition food and other supplies needed to ensure efficient operation.

(19) Supervise and coordinate activities of cooks and workers engaged in food preparation.

(20) Inspect supplies, equipment, and work areas to ensure conformance to established standards.

(21) Determine how food should be presented, and create decorative food displays.

(22) Instruct cooks and other workers in the preparation, cooking, garnishing, and presentation of food.

(23) Estimate amounts and costs of required supplies, such as food and ingredients.

(24) Collaborate with other personnel to plan and develop recipes and menus, taking into account such factors as seasonal availability of ingredients and the likely number of customers.

(25) Implement the hotel and department regulations, policies and procedures including but not limited to: House Rules and Regulation/Health and Safety/Grooming/Quality/Hygiene and Cleanliness.

(26) Perform related duties and special projects as assigned.

(27) Demonstrate awareness of all the policies and procedures and ensure all procedures are conducted safely and within the guidelines.

(28) Be aware of duty of care and adhere to occupational, health and safety legislation, policies and procedures.

(29) Be familiar with property safety, first aid and fire and emergency procedures and operate equipment safely and sensibly.

(30) Initiate action to correct a hazardous situation and notify supervisors of potential dangers.

(31) Log security incidents and accidents in accordance with hotel requirements.

(32) Coordinate and cooperate with fellow employees and seniors at all times.

(33) Ensure the smooth running of the outlet.

(34) Make employee roster as needed.

9. Doorman & Door Girl

Their job descriptions and responsibilities will include, but not limited to following.

(1) Make sure doors are open for every guest and they are properly greeted as per the hotel standard.

(2) Ensure that lobby area is clean, neat, and tidy.

(3) Give directions to the guest if necessary.

(4) Call porters or assist guest on their request.

(5) Call taxis if requested.

(6) Ensure that entrance to the hotel is always clear.

(7) Fond farewell to the guest in proper manner and as per the regulation.

(8) Ensure all the maintenance report are properly requested and followed up.

(9) Maintain standard of front of the house.

(10) Adhere with hotel emergency procedures.

(11) Complete knowledge of hotel layout and facilities.

(12) Be aware of special facilities/services for disabled people.

(13) Be aware of airport shuttle times.

(14) Assist guests and escort them to locations within the hotel at their request.

(15) Always comply with hotel procedures, rules and regulations on how to greet the customers.

(16) Follow safety policy at all times.

(17) Demonstrate Awareness of hotel policies and procedures and ensure all procedures are conducted safely and within the guidelines.

(18) Be aware of duty of care and adhere to occupational, health and safety legislation, policies and procedures.

(19) Be familiar with property safety, first aid and fire and emergency procedures and operate equipment safely and sensibly.

(20) Initiate action to correct a hazardous situation and notify supervisors of potential dangers.

(21) Adhere to Hotel Handbook and general policies and procedures.

(22) Provide information when requested and promotes hotel's service, facilities and special events.

(23) Anticipate guest needs, handle guest enquires, and solve problems.

(24) Create a positive hotel image in every interaction with internal and external customers.

(25) Adhere to hotel brand standards.

(26) Assist guests and escort them to locations within the hotel at their request.

(27) Demonstrate co-operation and trust with colleagues, supervisors, teams and across departments.

(28) Interact with department and hotel staff in a professional and positive manner to foster good rapport, promote team spirit and ensure two way communication effective.

(29) Be open to new ideas and make changes in the job and routine as required.

(30) Maximize opportunities for self development.

(31) Ensure that your work quality meets the standards required and complete tasks in a timely and thorough manner with minimum supervision.

(32) Follow standards, policies and procedures.

(33) Control or monitor parking or provide valet service (in some hotel).

10. Guest Relation Officer

Their responsibilities will include, but not be limited to the following.

(1) Greet, receive and conduct guests to tables, ensuring that they are properly attended to.

(2) Ensure that guests receive best courtesy while arriving at the hotel.

(3) Ensure that phone calls are answered within 3 rings and in proper phrase standardize by the hotel.

(4) Ensure that reservations are noted down properly (if necessary).

(5) Make sure entry door area is clean and tidy.

(6) Maintain the cleanliness of the hostess desk and surrounding area.

(7) Answers guests enquiries regarding food, service, charges, shows, promotional offers, etc.

(8) Accept and follow-up on table reservations as prescribed by existing procedures.

(9) Coordinate with Captain in making necessary arrangements according to floor plan for reservations, blocking off reserved tables, etc.

(10) Greet guest, escort them to their table, pull seat out for the ladies, and present menus.

(11) Channel complaints and suggestions to personnel concerned.

(12) Keep an eye on entire guests requests and follow up with server if necessary to make sure guest's requests are fulfilled.

(13) Assist in the maintenance of log book containing actual number of guests, covers, employees absence or on leave, guest's comments or complaints, etc.

(14) Offer amenities to guests after their meals.

(15) Maintain the condition of menus. Sort out soiled or torn menus and secure new ones whenever necessary, before each meal service.

(16) May be assigned to perform clerical duties such as typing and filing reports, memos and forms.

(17) May assist in the preparation of periodical reports and time sheets for the outlets.

(18) Comply with the hotel rules and follow the standard procedures.

(19) Adhere to hotel brand standards.

(20) Maintain hygiene at all times.

(21) Assist guests and escort them to locations within the hotel at their request.

(22) Communicate with other departments on guest requests and needs and create guest history and file it properly for future references.

(23) Monitor work done by maintenance or other departments as per the outlet request.

(24) Make sure of available and unavailable items in kitchen and mention it in briefing.

(25) Upgrade and arrange notice board at all times.

(26) Follow up all outgoing requests and upon its completion file it properly for future references.

(27) Monitor and upgrade log book, tip book or any other outlet communication book.

(28) Perform other F&B duties assigned by the captain or manager from time to time.

11. Banquet Servers

Banquet servers work for hotels, resorts, conference centers, caterers and restaurants. They are responsible for banquet functions and conferences. If the banquet halls are unoccupied then they might have to work in other food and beverage outlets. Their descriptions and responsibilities will include, but not limited to followings.

(1) Maintain personal hygiene, approach and uniform clean, neat and tidy as per the hotel standard.

(2) Set up the banquet room as specified by the customers.

(3) Make sure while moving chairs and tables follow the standard procedures.

(4) Set tables to laid-down standards, ensuring that all items used are clean, undamaged and in a good state of repair.

(5) Set up the table according to the hotel standard.

(6) Provide excellent food and beverage service for banquet events.

(7) Be totally familiar with the composition of all menu items.

(8) Serve food and beverages in accordance to the hotel standards, but above all in a professional, courteous manner.

(9) Explain the food or beverage if necessary.

(10) Assist customers if needed.

(11) Keep the buffet area neat and selections well stocked (If buffet only).

(12) Ensure sideboards on stations are adequately stocked with replacement cutlery, linen or other established needs, be they food or equipment.

(13) Ensure that soiled plates, cutleries, glasses are cleaned properly from the table and stock in well organized manner as per the hotel standard for the dishwashers.

(14) Ensure soiled lines are exchanged properly.

(15) Ensure banquet equipments are stored in appropriate places.

(16) Take inventory as per the hotel procedures and report to senior staff.

(17) Issue or report damage, maintenance, breakage promptly.

(18) Ensure that service standard are always maintained.

(19) Ensure food safety regulations are followed at all times.

(20) Prepare mise en place, refill side stations, and prepare table set ups.

(21) Serve beverage as per the functions requirement.

(22) Ensure beverage are served appropriately and follow hotel standard.

(23) Attend required training as per the outlet demands.

(24) Adhere hotel rules and regulations and follow standard procedures.

(25) Obtain necessary food handling and hygiene certificates.

(26) Maintain back of the house, front of the house, and side work duties for overall productivity of banquet events.

(27) Follow health and safety practices at all times.

Unit 5.4 Sequence of Service for Banquet

1. Dinner and Lunch

(1) Open the chair and assist with seating.

(2) Open the napkin and place on guest lap.

(3) Serve the mineral water from the right side.

(4) Serve the face towels from the right side.

(5) Serve the wine according the menu.

(6) Serve the bread and open the butter dish.

(7) Serve and clear the plates course by course.

(8) Offer red wine before you serve the main course.

(9) After clearance of the main course, clear B&B plates, salt and pepper shaker, butter dishes and bread basket.

(10) Remove the bread crumbs by using a clean side plate and service napkin.

(11) Open the dessert cutlery and serve the dessert.

(12) Before clearance of the dessert place the sugar and creamer.

(13) Clear the dessert plates and place the coffee cups.

(14) Serve the coffee and mignardise.

2. Service of Beverages

(1) Beverages will be served according the menu.

(2) Service will be proceeded always from the right side of the guest.

(3) Keep the bottle in the right hand & the service napkin in the left.

(4) After served one guest dry the bottle top with the napkin.

(5) Pay attention to the level of glasses (water half of the glass, white wine 2/3 of the glass, red wine 1/3 of the glass).

3. Service & Clearance of Food

(1) Food service will be proceeded from the right hand side of the guest (except silver service, sauce service and bread service).

(2) Never carry more than 2 plates.

(3) We serve ladies first, than gents.

(4) Service and clearance will be proceeded table wise and together.

(5) Clearance not before every guest on the table is finished with eating.

(6) Every waiter will serve his allocated positions.

(7) Service will be proceeded clock wise.

4. Do and Don't Do

(1) Smile! The guest will never forget the smile.

(2) Serve and clear always from the right side.

(3) Use the guest name if possible.

(4) Help the guests with putting and getting up. Lady's first.

(5) Service always moves clockwise around the table.

(6) Use the tray. It is your best friend!

(7) In hard times the nerves never lose and remain kind.

(8) Communicate with the team members to offer the best possible service.

(9) The service will be continued until the last guest leaves the room.

(10) Fulfill every need of the guest with self-initiative.

5. Don't

(1) Never say "No"!

(2) Never give the guest an excuse!

(3) Never bring an incomplete order to the table!

(4) Nothing is stacked on tables and side stations!

(5) Ask never the guests: who gets what?

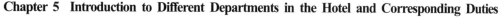

(6) Never lean or rest in front of the guest!

(7) Let the fingers from the face and the hair!

(8) Never come to work in bad mood! The guests notice it immediately and your colleagues hate it.

(9) Never doubt about a standard!

(10) Keep your mobile phone switched off during your work.

(11) Don't eat in the back of the house area.

Appendix A

Useful Vocabulary in Interviews

A

ability *n.*

She has no ability in that kind of work.

她没有做那种工作的能力。

academic *adj.*

The university is composed of five academic schools.

整个大学由 5 个学院组成。

acceptable *adj.*

The terms of the contract are acceptable to us.

我们认为这个合同的条件可以接受。

accomplishment *n.*

Her technical accomplishment on the piano is startling.

她在钢琴方面的造诣令人惊叹。

achieve *v.*

Only practice can achieve mastery.

只有实践才能达到精通。

adapt *v.*

She knew how to adapt herself to the environment.

她懂得如何适应环境。

adaptability *n.*

adaptability and sense of humor is needed.

适应能力和幽默感是必须的。

adequate *adj.*

Though a bit too old, he is still adequate to the work.

虽然他年纪大了点，却仍能胜任这项工作。

adept *adj.*

He is an adept mechanic.

他是一个熟练的机械师。

additional *adj.*

Guests have to pay additional charges for their extra beverages.

客人们另外点的饮料要额外付费。

admire *v.*

We admire his working so hard.

我们钦佩他工作努力。

advantage *n.*

It would advantage you to work hard.

努力工作对你会有益。

affect *v.*

The tax increases have affected us all.

加税已经影响了我们所有的人。

ambition *n.*

His ambition knows no limits.

他的野心是无止尽的。

ambitious *adj.*
She is ambitious to succeed.
她极想成功。

apathetic *adj.*
You won't succeed if you are apathetic.
要是你缺乏兴趣，你就不能成功。

appeal (to) *n.*
We made an appeal to the employees for money to build the bridge.
为了建造这座桥，我们呼吁员工捐款。

apply (for/ to) *v.*
We should try to learn economic theory and apply it.
我们应努力学习经济理论并能应用。

assign *v.*
They have assigned me a small room.
他们已给我分配了一个小房间。

application *n.*
He has filed his application.
他已经呈交了申请书。

applicant *n.*
As the wages were low, there were few applicants for the job.
因为工资低，没有什么人申请这份工作。

appraise *v.*
The interviewer appraised the pupil's performance.
面试官评价了那个学生的表现。

appropriate *adj.*
It is appropriate that he should get the post.
由他担任这一职务是恰当的。

assess *v.*
We should equitably assess his performance.
我们应该公正地评价他的表现。

assit *v.*
How may I assist you?
我能帮您做什么呢?

assiatance *n.*
I`m just glad to be of assistance
我很高兴能帮上忙。

attendance *n.*
The attendance of this class never dropped off.
这个班的出席人数从未下降。

attire *n.*
He had no intention of changing his mode of attire.
他无意改变着装方式。

attitude *n.*
What's your attitude to/towards this idea?
你对这种意见看法如何？

autonomy *n.*
Branch managers have full autonomy in their own areas.
分支机构的经理在其管辖范围内有充分的自主权。

available *adj.*
The rest room is not available, and it is being repaired.
洗手间现在不能用，因为正在修理。

award *n.* / *v.*
They awarded John the first prize.
他们授予约翰一等奖。

B

background *n.*
She has a background in child psychology.
她受过儿童心理学的教育。

bearing *n.*
He is a man of erect and soldierly bearing *adj.*

他是一个身子挺直、具有军人风度的男子。

behavior *n.*

A person's behavior is often regulated by his circumstances.

人的行为常受其所处环境的约束。

benefit *n. / v.*

That was a health program to benefit everyone.

那是一项对人人都有好处的健康计划。

briefly *adv.*

I want to touch briefly on another aspect of the problem.

我想简单地谈一下这个问题的另一方面。

broad-minded *adj.*

He is broad-minded.

他心胸坦荡。

C

campus *n.*

The campus of Harvard University is very beautiful.

哈佛大学的校园非常漂亮。

candidate *n.*

He interviews many candidates for jobs.

他面试过很多求职者。

capable *adj.*

Jim is capable at sports.

吉姆擅长运动。

career *n.*

My uncle entered upon a diplomatic career at the age of thirty-five.

我伯父 35 岁时开始了外交官的生涯。

caring *adj.*

Children need a caring environment.

儿童需要一个受关怀的环境。

category *n.*

These form an independent category.

这些形成了一个独立的种类。

certificate *n.*

These are my ID card, diploma and my certificate for accountant qualifications.

这是我的身份证、毕业证书和会计资格证书。

challenge *v.*

The job doesn't really challenge him.

这项工作不能真正地考验他。

challenging *adj.*

She performed the most challenging task without a mistake.

她毫无差错地完成了这一最富有挑战性的任务。

cheerful *adj.*

He is cheerful in spite of his illness.

尽管他生病了，但精神很好。

client *n.*

She can't come to the telephone, she's serving a client.

她不能来接电话，她正在接待一位顾客。

colleague *n.*

He is a colleague of mine.

他是我的同事。

collaborate *v.*

The work gets done more quickly when we collaborate.

当我们协作时，工作做起来会更快。

comment *v.*

I won't comment on what people say.

对人们说的话我不作评论。

communicate *v.*

A politician must be able to communicate.

政治家必须善于表达自己的观点。

communicative *adj.*

He has a headache and isn't feeling communicative today.

他今天头痛，不爱说话。

communication *n.*

Telegraph communication was broken off.

电讯中断了。

competence *n.*

We knew her competence in solving problems.

我们都知道她解决问题的能力。

competent *adj.*

He did a competent job.

他的工作做得相当出色。

competition *n.*

There is keen competition between the two motorcar firms.

两家汽车公司之间存在激烈的竞争。

comprehension *n.*

The teacher set the class a comprehension test.

老师对全班同学进行了一次理解力测验。

conceivable *adj.*

It is conceivable that there will be a new economic crisis throughout the world, but we hope it won't happen.

人们相信一场新的经济危机可能再次席卷全球，但是我们希望它不要发生。

concern *n.* / *v.*

The second question concerns our method of work.

第二个问题牵涉到我们的工作方法。

conference *n.*

Nearly all the members attended the conference.

几乎全体成员都出席了这次会议。

conflict *n.*

Your statement is in conflict with the rest of the evidence.

你的陈述同其余证据有矛盾。

confuse *v.*

They asked so many questions that they confused me.

他们问了许多问题，都把我弄糊涂了。

confused *adj.*

All your changes of plan have made me totally confused.

你把计划改来改去，我都糊涂了。

conscientious *adj.*

He is a conscientious student.

他是一个勤奋的学生。

considerable *adj.*

They have given the plan considerable attention.

他们已经给予这个计划以相当多的关注。

consideration *n.*

We shall give your request our fullest consideration.

我们会认真考虑你的请求。

constructive *adj.*

We welcome constructive criticism.

我们乐意接受有建设性的批评。

contribute *v.*

I just can contribute 100 dollars.

我充其量只能捐助 100 美元。

contribution *n.*

This is the contribution to the hotel.

这是对酒店的贡献。

cooperate *v.*

We hope we can cooperate even more closely

in the future.
希望我们今后能更加密切地合作。

cooperative *adj.*

We thank you for your cooperative efforts.
我们感谢你方的努力合作。

core *n.*

The core of our appeal is freedom of speech.
我们呼吁的中心是要言论自由。

count *v.*

Quality counts above origin.
质量比产地更重要。

course *n.*

The college course was then cut to three years.
之后大学学制缩短到3年。

courteous *adj.*

Although she often disagreed with me, she was always courteous.
尽管她常常和我意见不一，但她总是很谦恭有礼。

creative *adj.*

He is a very creative boss.
他是一个非常有创造力的老板。

creativity *n.*

There is limited scope for creativity in my job.
在我的工作中发挥创造力的空间有限。

credibility *n.*

Recommendations from two previous clients helped to establish her credibility.
两位以前的客户的推荐有助于确立她的诚信度。

criticize *v.*

Hey, don't ever criticize my idol.
不要这样批评我的偶像。

criticism *n.*

Some youth today do not allow any criticism at all.
现在有些年轻人根本指责不得。

cultivate *v.*

She cultivated her mind by reading many books.
她博览群书，修身养性。

current *adj.*

They suggested measures to overcome current difficulties.
他们提出了克服目前困难的措施。

customer *n.*

These goods enjoy growing favor among the customers.
这些货物越来越受顾客的欢迎。

D

deal *v.*

He must deal with many difficulties.
他必须应付许多困难。

defect *n.*

We must correct our defects as soon as possible.
我们必须尽快纠正我们的缺点。

define *v.*

Please define the words.
请定义这些词。

definition *n.*

I made a definition for this position.
我给这个职位下了一个定义。

demerit *n.*

Each man has his merits and demerits.
每个人都有他的优点和缺点。

demonstrate *v.*

Recent events demonstrate the need of change in policy.

最近的事态表明政策需要改变。

demonstration *n.*

His new book is a demonstration of his patriotism.

他写的新书是他的爱国精神的证明。

dependable *adj.*

She is loyal and totally dependable.

她很忠诚，完全值得信赖。

describe *v.*

Can you describe it to me?

你能把它描述给我听吗?

desire *n. / v.*

The workers desire better working conditions.

工人们要求更好的工作条件。

detail *n.*

If you're interested in the job, I'll send you all the details.

如果你对这份工作感兴趣，我将给你发送所有详细资料。

determined *adj.*

As he was not reconciled to his defeat, he was determined to try again in the next contest.

他不甘心这次失败，决心参加下次比赛。

diligent *adj.*

He is diligent in whatever he does.

他无论做什么都很勤奋。

diligence *n.*

Care and diligence bring luck.

谨慎勤奋，带来好运。

dimension *n.*

There is another dimension to this problem which you haven't considered.

这个问题还有你尚未考虑到的另一方面。

diploma *n.*

She worked hard to earn her music diploma.

她刻苦用功，以求获得音乐学位证书。

disadvantage *n.*

We were put at a serious disadvantage.

我们被置于非常不利的地位。

discipline *n.*

She needs the discipline of having to write an essay every week.

她需要进行每周写一篇文章的训练。

disciplined *adj.*

Be more disciplined!

注意纪律!

discreet *adj.*

He is very discreet in giving his opinions.

发表意见时他十分慎重。

donate *v.*

They used to donate large sum of money to the Red Cross every year.

他们过去每年都向红十字会捐献大笔的钱。

donation *n.*

They made a generous donation to charity.

他们对慈善事业慷慨捐助。

drawback *n.*

Everything has its drawback.

凡事皆有不足之处。

E

education *n.*

I'm looking for a little background about the English education system.

我想了解一下英国教育体制的情况。

effect *n.*

Have the English classes any effect on her?

上英语班对她有什么效果吗?

effective *adj.*

These are effective measures.

这些都是有效的措施。

efficient *adj.*

She is an efficient manageress.

她是一个有能力的经理。

energetic *adj.*

He is always energetic.

他总是精力旺盛。

enterprising *adj.*

Phil is an enterprising cook.

菲尔是个有进取心的厨师。

entertainment *n.*

The hotel is famous for its entertainment.

这家旅馆以殷勤待客而著称。

enthusiasm *n.*

One of his many enthusiasms is a great fondness of eastern music.

酷爱东方音乐是他的众多爱好之一。

enthusiastic *adj.*

I gathered from the way she replied that she wasn't very enthusiastic.

从她回答的语气判断，我觉得她不是很热心。

essential *adj.*

It is essential for us to know all the facts.

对我们来说，了解所有的事实是必要的。

establish *v.*

We have established close relations with many companies.

我们已和许多公司建立了密切的关系。

etiquette *n.*

He understands about diplomatic etiquette.

他熟知外交礼节。

evaluate *v.*

I can't evaluate his ability without seeing his work.

没有看到他的工作情况，我无法评估他的能力。

evaluation *n.*

I attempted an honest evaluation of my own life.

我试图如实地评价我自己的一生。

evidence *n.*

There wasn't enough evidence to prove him guilty.

没有充分的证据证明他有罪。

excellent *adj.*

The student was excellent in chemistry.

这个学生的化学成绩优异。

excellence *n.*

She turned out to be an organizer par excellence.

结果表明她是个优秀的组织者。

exceed *v.*

The demand for skilled engineer exceeds the supply this month.

本月工程师职位供不应求。

except *prep.*

He could do little except write.

他除了会写之外，其他什么都不行。

exception *n.*

Every rule has its exception.

一切规则皆有例外。

exceptional *adj.*

Our circumstances have been rather

exceptional.
我们的情况相当特别。

expect *v.*

She expects to fail the interview.
她预料无法通过面试。

expectation *n.*

His parents have great expectations for his future.
他父母对他的前途寄予厚望。

experience *n. / v.*

Experience is the best teacher.
经验是最好的老师。

experienced *adj.*

Seek for an experienced employee to fill the post.
找一位有经验的员工来担当此职。

expectation *n.*

His parents have great expectations for his future.
他父母对他的前途深寄厚望。

expection *n.*

Our expection depend on you.
我们的希望寄托在你身上

express *v.*

He expressed his views at the meeting.
他在会上发表了自己的观点。

expression *n.*

All their expressions were not true.
他们的所有表情都不是真的。

extra *adj.*

Room service is extra.
房价不含小费。

extracurricular *adj.*

Most of the students in the class take an active part in extracurricular.
班上绝大部分学生都积极参加课外活动。

extremely *adv.*

Outwardly she looked confident but in reality she felt extremely nervous.
表面上她显得很自信，其实她非常紧张。

eye contact *n.*

Appropriate eye contact is also important socially.
恰当的目光交流对社会交往也是很重要的。

F

factor *n.*

Industry and modesty are the chief factors of his success.
勤奋和谦虚是他成功的主要因素。

failure *n.*

Failure teaches success.
失败是成功之母。

fear *n./ v.*

They feared the worst.
他们担心会发生最坏的情况。

figure *n./ v.*

The above figure did not include workers.
上面的数字没有包括工人。

flexible *adj.*

He has a flexible mind.
他脑瓜灵活。

fluency *n.*

Fluency in spoken English is essential.
能讲一口流利的英语很重要。

fluent *adj.*

She speaks fluent English.

她说一口流利的英语。

fluently *adv.*

I can speak Mandarin fluently.

我能说流利的普通话。

focus *n. / v.*

She was the focus of everyone's attention.

她是大家关注的焦点。

fraud *n.*

I saw through the fraud.

我识破了那个骗局。

friendly *adj.*

They are on friendly terms with the boss.

他们与老板的关系融洽。

friendliness *n.*

His manner was a blend of friendliness and respect.

他的态度友善且毕恭毕敬。

frustrate *v.*

The bad weather frustrated all our hopes of going out.

恶劣的天气破坏了我们出行的愿望。

frustrating *adj.*

It was a demeaning and ultimately frustrating experience.

那是一次有失颜面并且令人沮丧至极的经历。

G

genuine *adj.*

His wish to help seems genuine.

看来他是真诚地想给予帮助。

gesture *n.*

He made a rude gesture with his fingers.

他用手指做了一个不礼貌的手势。

groom *v.*

Duff is being groomed for the job of manager.

达夫正在接受训练，准备当经理。

groom *v.*

He is grooming his son for the directorship of the firm

他准备推荐自己的儿子担任公司的经理。

H

handle *v.*

Do you know how to handle the machine?

你知道怎样操作这台机器吗?

hardworking *adj.*

He was incompetent yet hardworking.

他能力较弱，但工作还是勤勤恳恳的。

harm *n./ v.*

Smoking harms our health.

吸烟有害健康。

harmful *adj.*

It is conspicuous that smoking is harmful to health.

很明显，抽烟对健康有害。

harmony *n.*

His ideas were no longer in harmony with ours.

他的想法同我们的不再一致了。

harmonious *adj.*

They can build a more harmonious society once inequality and exploitation are removed.

消除了不平等与剥削，他们就能建立一个更为和谐的社会。

helpful *adj.*

Our teacher gave us a lot of helpful books in maths.

我们老师给了我们许多在数学上有帮助

的书。

hire *v.*

We hired a driver to take us on a tour of the city.

我们雇了一个司机带我们游览这个城市。

hobby *n.*

He entered into politics as a hobby.

他参加政治活动是作为一种业余爱好。

honest *adj.*

He was very honest to tell me his story.

他十分坦率地给我讲了他的故事。

honesty *n.*

I can't in all honesty say that I've had much experience of this kind of work, but I'm willing to try it.

说实话，我在这方面并没有多少工作经验，但我很想试一试。

humor *n.*

He has a sense of humor.

他具有一种幽默感。

humorous *adj.*

He is a humorous salesman.

他是一位幽默的推销员。

I

ideal *n./ adj.*

She's looking for a job but hasn't found her ideal yet.

她在寻找一份工作，但迄今为止还没有找到理想的。

image *n.*

I have this image of you as always being cheerful and optimistic.

你留给我的印象总是快活和乐观。

immaculate *adj.*

Her apartment was immaculate.

她的公寓房间洁净无垢。

implement *v.*

Before you implement your plans, you must have a profound knowledge of markets there.

在你实施计划之前.你必须深入了解那里的市场。

impression *n.*

She made a good impression on her boss.

她给老板留下了很好的印象。

inspire *v.*

His speech inspired the crowd.

他的演说鼓舞了群众。

include *v.*

Their course of study includes elementary hygiene and medical theory.

他们的课程包括基础卫生学和医疗知识。

income *n.*

What's your expected income?

你期望的收入是多少？

indifferent *adj.*

His manner was cold and indifferent.

他的态度既冷淡又无动于衷。

indispensable *adj.*

For a successful class humor is indispensable.

要在课堂上取得成功，幽默是必不可少的。

influence *n./ v.*

Her influence made me a better person.

她对我的影响使我成为一个更好的人

influential *adj.*

He is a very influential man in the company.

他在公司中是个很有影响的人物。

innovate *v.*

We must innovate in order to make progress.
我们必须改革以便取得进步。

interpersonal *adj.*

Interpersonal communication is necessary.
人际沟通是必要的。

interview *n./ v.*

Don't be late for your job interview.
求职面试不能迟到。

interviewee *n.*

When you are interviewee, surely, you should pay attention to the interviewer's eyes.
当然，在面试时，记住要看着考官的眼睛。

interviewer *n.*

Always maintain eye contact with the interviewer.
和雇主要一直保持目光接触。

issue *n.*

There was no issue at all between us.
我们之间毫无争议。

K

key (to) *n.*

I don't know the key to the answer.
我不知道这个问题的答案。

L

leadership *n.*

The leadership of the movement is in agreement on this issue.
这一运动的领导层对这个问题的看法一致。

likeable *adj.*

She is likeable enough, but very ordinary.
她还算可爱，但实在没什么特别的风韵。

logical *adj.*

It is logical that the book is expensive.
书贵是很自然的事。

loyal *adj.*

He is a loyal staff.
他是一位忠诚的职员。

loyalty *n.*

If the interviewer asked about your family or school, you should speak with loyalty and affection.
当面试官提到你的家庭和学校时，你说话时要显得忠诚和热爱。

luxury *adj.*

This is a luxury hotel
这是一个豪华的饭店

M

maintain *v.*

The two companies have maintained friendly relations for many years.
两个公司多年来一直保持着友好的关系。

manner *n.*

Good manner will leave a good impression to the employers.
良好的举止会给面试官留下好印象。

mature *adj.*

The new manager is more mature than his predecessor.
新经理比他的前任更成熟一些。

mention *v.*

He did not want to mention the painful past.
他不愿意提起过去的伤心事。

merit *n.*

There is great merit in dealing fairly with your employees.

公正地对待你的雇员有极大好处。

mission *n.*

The minister was sent to Spain on mission.

这位部长奉命前往西班牙。

misunderstand *v.*

Don't misunderstand what I'm trying to say.

别误解我要说的话。

misunderstanding

I don't want any misunderstanding.

我不希望有任何误解。

modest *adj.*

He is a very modest person.

他是一位非常谦逊的人。

motivate *v.*

No one really knows what motivated him to do so.

没有人确实知道他那样做的动机。

motivation *n.*

The motivation for the decision is the desire to improve our service to our customers.

做这个决定的动机是希望改善我们对顾客的服务。

motivated *adj.*

Employees are motivated to work harder for a whole host of different reasons.

促使雇员更加努力工作的原因多种多样。

N

native *adj*

He read a poem in his native language.

他用母语朗读了一首诗。

nervous *adj*

She felt very nervous with so many people looking at her.

这么多人瞧着她，她感到非常紧张。

numerous *adj*

There are numerous people in the square.

有许多人在广场上。

O

opportunity *n.*

He sought opportunities of doing her little service.

他寻找机会为她尽一点力。

optimistic *adj.*

He is an optimistic young fellow.

他是一位乐观的年轻人。

organize *v.*

He has the ability to organize.

他很有组织才能。

orientated *adj.*

The course was orientated towards foreign students.

该课程是专为外国学生开的.

orientation *n.*

New employees need some orientation when they go to work.

新员工上班前需要培训。

outgoing *adj.*

He is an outgoing and lively person.

他是一个性格开朗而又活泼的人。

overcome *v.*

He has enough courage to overcome the difficulty.

他有足够的勇气来克服这个困难。

P

particular *adj.*

This is a particular account of the accident.

这是一份全面而详尽的事故报告。

passion *n.*

He could not control his passion.

他无法控制自己的激情。

patient *adj.*

Facing the trouble he is patient.

面对麻烦时他表现得很有耐心。

patience *n.*

We haven't the patience to hear such an empty talk.

我们可没耐心去听这种空谈。

pay *v.*

This job pays well.

这份工作报酬不错。

payment *n.*

I gave ten pounds in payment for the goods I bought.

我买那些东西付了 10 英镑。

pay-scale *n.*

Are you familiar with our pay-scale?

你清楚我们的工资级别吗?

perfect *adj.*

His technique is almost perfect.

他的技巧近乎完美。

perfection *n.*

His performance was sheer perfection.

他的表演达到了尽善尽美的地步。

perform *v.*

He always performs his duty faithfully.

他一贯忠实地履行自己的职责。

performance *n.*

The pianist gave a fine performance.

钢琴家演奏得很出色。

personality *n.*

His personality is in good taste.

他的品格很高尚。

persuade *v.*

It is easy to persuade oneself.

说服自己往往很容易。

pertain to *v.*

The inspector was interested in everything pertaining to the school.

视察员对有关学校的一切都感兴趣。

pleasant *adj.*

It is pleasant for us to meet you.

遇见你我们感到很高兴。

polite *adj.*

I've never seen such a polite clerk.

我从未见过这样有礼貌的店员。

politeness *n.*

It's no more than common politeness to hear what she has to say.

听她说话只不过是出于基本的礼貌。

position *n.*

What do you see as the priorities for someone in this position?

你在招聘的这个职位的工作人员时优先考虑哪些条件?

positive *adj.*

I am positive that I can win.

我敢肯定我能赢。

posture *n.*

He bid us keep in a ready posture.

他嘱咐我们做好准备。

Potential *adj*

It's important to draw out employees' potential

capacities.
发掘员工的潜在能力是很重要的。

present *v.*
How many of the group are present today?
今天该组有多少人出席?

presentation *n.*
His presentation was clear and incisive.
他的报告清晰而犀利。

pressure *n.*
He changed his mind under the pressure from his boss.
他在老板的逼迫之下改变了主意。

previous *adj.*
The author mentioned it in the previous paragraph.
作者在前一段里提到这件事。

prize *n.*
He received his prize with a proud step.
他骄傲地走去领奖。

profession *n.*
Medicine is her destined profession.
医学是她命中注定要从事的职业。

professional *adj.*
She is a professional actress.
她是职业演员。

profit *n.*
What's the profit of doing that?
那样做有什么好处呢?

progress *n.*
During these years the service of this hotel has made great progress.
这些年来，这个酒店的服务改进不少。

project *v.*
Can you project a new working scheme for us?
你能为我们设计一个新的工作计划吗?

promote *v.*
My son's just been promoted.
我儿子刚被提拔。

promotion *n.*
Promotion in the job was by seniority.
这种工作得按资历晋升。

proposal *n.*
They presented concrete proposals for improvement.
他们提出了具体的改进建议。

prospective *adj.*
Is she a prospective buyer?
她可能成为我们的顾客吗?

proud *adj.*
We are proud for you to win the championship.
我们为你赢得冠军而骄傲。

punctual *adj.*
I am not myself a particularly punctual person.
我本人不是一个严守时间的人。

pursue *v.*
He began to pursue an easy and comfortable life.
他开始追求安逸舒适的生活。

Q

quality *n.*
Sympathy is his best quality.
具有同情心是他最好的品质。

qualify *v.*
I won't qualify until next year.
我明年才具备资格。

qualified (for) *adj.*
Jane is well qualified for this teaching job.
简很适合担任这份教职。

qualification *n.*

You have all qualifications to do the job.

你有资格做这份工作。

quality *n.*

Sympathy is his best quality.

同情心是他最好的品质。

quantity *n.*

What quantity do you require?

你要求多大的数量?

R

range *n.*

Several rooms are available within this price range.

在这个价格范围内，有几个房间可供选择。

reaction *n.*

Their reaction to the joke is to laugh.

他们对这个笑话的反应是笑。

recommend *v.*

Can you recommend a classmate who can take up the job?

你能不能推荐一位能承担这项工作的同学？

recommendation *n.*

I wrote him a good recommendation.

我为他写了一封很好的推荐信。

relate *v.*

His remarks didn't relate to the topic under discussion.

他说的话与讨论的问题无关。

reliable *adj.*

The manager thought he was a reliable person and told him all about the new plan.

经理认为他是一个可靠的人，并把关于新计划的全部内容都告诉了他。

religion *n.*

There are many religions in the world.

在世界上有许多种宗教。

religious *adj.*

She is a very religious person who goes to church every Sunday.

她十分虔诚，每星期都上教堂。

relocate *v.*

They've relocated our bus-stop.

他们把我们的公共汽车站迁到另一个位置了。

remuneration *n.*

He received a generous remuneration for his services.

他收到一笔丰厚的劳务酬金。

renown *n.*

His renown has spread throughout the country.

他的名声已传遍全国。

repeated *adj.*

After repeated attempts they finally succeeded.

经过反复尝试，他们终于成功了。

resource *n.*

This country is rich in natural resources.

该国自然资源丰富。

resourceful *adj.*

He is very clever and endlessly resourceful.

他聪明机敏、足智多谋。

responsible *adj.*

She is a responsible secretary.

她是一个尽职尽责的秘书。

responsibility *n.*

He has no responsibility for that accident.

他对那个事故没有责任。

resume *n.*

He resumed his former position with the company.

他又恢复了在公司的职位。

S

salary *n.*

He was engaged at a salary of 1000 a month.

他以月薪一千美元受聘。

satisfy *v.*

Nothing can always satisfy.

没有任何东西能总是使人满足。

satisfied *adj.*

When she had finished her meal, she gave a satisfied smile.

当她吃完饭后，她露出了满意的笑容。

satisfactory *adj.*

Sales are very satisfactory this month.

本月销售情况令人十分满意。

schoolmate *n.*

When his schoolmate made the last goal, the boy gave out with an untrammeled yell.

那个男孩在他的同学踢进最后一球时不禁纵声欢呼。

self-introduction *n.*

Let me make a self-introduction first.

首先让我来自我介绍一下。

self-motivated *adj.*

He is mature, self-motivated and strong interpersonal skills.

他思想成熟、上进心强，并且具有极其丰富的人际关系技巧。

self-disciplined *adj.*

I have the ability to work independently and self-disciplined.

我有独立工作能力及自律能力。

seize *v.*

Gill seized my hand and shook it heartily.

吉尔突然抓住我的手，热情地和我握手。

sensitive *adj.*

Don't be so sensitive—I wasn't criticizing you.

别这么神经质——我不是在批评你。

short-coming *n.*

What's your shortcoming?

你的缺点是什么？

sign *v.*

When we arrive at the office each morning we have to sign on the dotted line.

我们每天早上到达办公室的时候，得在签到簿上签到。

signature *n.*

These two signatures are very similar, can you tell them apart?

这两处签名非常接近，你能把它们区分开来吗？

significant *adj.*

Your success today may be significant for your whole future.

你今天的成功对你的整个将来可能都是有意义的。

sincere *adj.*

His apology was sincere.

他的歉意是出自内心的。

sincerely *adv.*

I sincerely hope that you will be successful.

我衷心祝愿你成功。

sincerity *n.*

He tried hard to satisfy me of his sincerity.

他竭力让我了解他的诚意。

skill *n.*

He has skill in painting.

他擅长绘画。

sloppy *adj.*

She's always criticizing her staff for being sloppy.

她总是指责她的下属做事马虎。

slovenly *adj.*

Don't slouch in that slovenly way!

别那么没精打彩！

specific *adj.*

Will you be specific?

请讲清楚些，好吗？

statement *n.*

The government issued a statement urging the public to cooperate in this inquiry.

政府发表声明要公众对这项调查给予配合。

stimulate *v.*

They stimulated me to make greater efforts.

他们鼓励我要做出更大的努力。

strategy *n.*

By careful strategy she negotiated a substantial pay rise.

她精心策划后，谈妥了大幅增加工资的事。

strength *n.*

Tolerance is one of his strengths.

宽容是他的一个优点。

strengthen *v.*

We should strengthen discipline.

我们应该加强纪律。

strong point *n.*

Dancing is not her strong point.

她不擅长跳舞。

subject *n.*

We didn't get to the core of the subject.

我们没触及问题的核心。

successful *adj.*

She is a successful businesswoman.

她是一位很成功的女实业家。

summary *n.*

He made a summary of what had been done.

他总结了所做的事情。

supervisor *n.*

He said that he needed to get his supervisor to authorize my refund.

他说必须让主管人员批准我的退款。

T

tactful *adj.*

Remember to be tactful when expressing a personal judgment.

记住表达个人看法要婉转。

teamwork *n.*

Only teamwork will enable us to get the job done on time.

只有团结一致，我们才能按时完成这项工作。

trait *n.*

His generosity is one of his good traits.

慷慨大方是他的优秀品质之一。

train *v.*

They trained him as an engineer.

他们把他培养成一名工程师。

trainee *n.*

He joined the company as a graduate trainee.

他毕业后到这个公司当过实习生。

trainer *n.*

Our trainer had a strong influence on the team.

我们的教练对这个队的影响很大。

training *n.*
I haven't had any real training.
我没有受过什么真正的训练。

trustworthy *adj.*
It is generally admitted that he is a trustworthy person.
大家一致公认他是一个可信赖的人。

U

union *n.*
Union between the two companies would be impossible.
这两个公司的联合是不可能的。

V

vision *n.*
I've had my eyes tested and the report says that my vision is perfect.
我去检查眼睛，根据报告我视力极佳。

virtue *n.*
Among her many virtues are loyalty, courage, and truthfulness.
她有许多的美德，如忠诚、勇敢和诚实。

W

weak point *n.*
My weak point is that I am short of work experience.
我的劣势是缺乏工作经验。

weakness *n.*
He admitted his weakness.
他承认自己的短处。

Appendix B

A Brief Introduction to Worldwide Renowned Hotel Groups

Our training is mainly focused on the interview for overseas hotels. Here we are going to share a brief introduction to the history, culture, philosophy and brands of some worldwide renowned hotel groups as follows.

(1) Jumeirah Hotels & Resorts;

(2) Intercontinental Hotels Group;

(3) Acccor Hotels & Resorts;

(4) Hilton Worldwide;

(5) Starwood Hotels and Resorts.

1. Jumeirah Hotels & Resorts (Stay Different)

(1) History. Jumeirah Hotels & Resorts belongs to Jumeirah group, which is regarded as among the most luxurious and innovative hotel group in the world and has won numerous international travel and tourism awards. The company was founded in 1997 with the aim to become a hospitality industry leader through establishing a world class portfolio of luxury hotels and resorts.

Jumeirah Beach Hotel redefined what a luxury destination could be. Then came Burj Al Arab, Jumeirah—the most luxurious hotel in the world. By 2000 Jumeirah Emirates Towers was receiving accolades from business travellers. Two legendary London Hotels – Jumeirah Carlton Tower and the Jumeirah Lowndes Hotel in Belgravia was rejuvenated. By 2004 Madinat Jumeirah (three grand boutique hotels forming an Arabian city) had risen on Dubai's waterfront. Then Jumeirah Bab Al Shams Desert Resort & Spa appeared like a mirage in the dunes. By 2006 we were busy in New York transforming Jumeirah Essex House into one of the most magnificent hotels in America.

Jumeirah Group's main activity is operating luxury hotels and resorts, it also manages Jumeirah Living, a luxury brand of serviced residences; Talise, the spa brand; Jumeirah Restaurants, the restaurant division; the thrilling Wild Wadi Waterpark; the Emirates Academy of Hospitality Management; and Jumeirah Retail, which runs 15 stores.

(2) Brands and locations.

Dubai:

Burj Al Arab

Jumeirah Beach Hotel

Jumeirah Emirates Towers, Madinat Jumeirah, Jumeirah Bab Al Shams Desert Resort & Spa, Jumeirah The Meydan, Jumeirah Zabeel Saray

London: Jumeirah Carlton, Jumeirah Lowndes Hotel

New York: Jumeirah Essex House

(3) Culture & philosophy.

Core essence: STAY DIFFERENT

Hallmarks:

1 I will always smile and greet our guests before they greet me.

2 My first response to a guest request will never be no.

3 I will treat all colleagues with respect and integrity.

Jumeirah guiding principles & vision:

Integrity: We act with honesty and sincerity in everything we do. We say what we mean, do what we say and build confidence in our team.

Teamwork: We work towards common goals through open communication, mutual support and win-win attitudes. We respect our differences and build upon our strengths.

Recognition: We ensure that people's individual needs and successes are supported and recognized.

Innovation: We are open minded, challenging conventional thinking, improving our processes and implementing new ideas faster than our competitors.

Continuous Growth: We provide an environment where our colleagues and our business can flourish and grow.

People Focus: We focus on our colleagues, customers and business associates and they acknowledge us as preferred partners.

Our Vision: To be a world class luxury international hotel and hospitality management company, committed to being the industry leader in all of our activities through dedication to our stakeholders; colleagues, customers, business partners and owners.

2. Intercontinental Hotels Group (IHG)

(1) History. IHG is an international hotel company whose goal is to create Great Hotels Guests Love. It has more guest rooms than any other hotel company in the world—that's more than 650000 rooms and over 4500 hotels in 100 countries and territories around the world.

From the first Bass brewery in 1777 to today's hotel company with more guest rooms than any other, IHG's history is one of pioneering people and new ideas.

1777 William Bass sets up a brewery in Burton-on-Trent. The Bass business thrives, developing into one of the UK's leading brewers.

1876 The Bass red triangle becomes the first trademark to be registered in the UK.

1960s Bass acquires a number of well-known regional brewing companies including Mitchells & Butlers in the Midlands (1961), before merging with Charringtons in London in 1967. These acquisitions make Bass one of the largest brewers and pub owners in the UK.

1988 Bass makes its first significant international move into the hotel industry, buying Holiday Inns International.

1989 The Beer Orders legislation is passed. This limits the number of tied pubs that major brewers can own and signals a major industry restructuring.

Bass reduces the number of pubs that it owns dramatically and focuses on larger outlets. At the same time, it directs cashflow into developing an international hotel business.

1990 Bass buys the North American Holiday Inn business and Holiday Inn grows internationally.

1991 Bass launches Holiday Inn Express, a complementary brand in the limited service segment.

1994 Bass launches Crowne Plaza, a move into the upscale hotel market.

CROWNE PLAZA
HOTELS & RESORTS

Bass's pubs business continues to grow. The business has also become increasingly branded. Bass opens the first O'Neill's public house in 1994 and acquires the restaurant chain Harvester in September 1995.

The Harvester acquisition, the development of the All Bar One brand in 1994 and the acquisition of the Browns restaurant chain marks a significant commitment to the growing eating out market in the UK.

1996 Bass's attempt to acquire half of the Carlsberg-Tetley brewing business in the UK is blocked by the UK government. Bass renews its focus on its hotels and pubs divisions. Over the next few years, it sells smaller, non-core businesses such as Gala bingo and Coral bookmakers, along with some of its pubs, including the leased pub business.

1997 As the hotel business becomes more purely brand focused, Bass sells its North American midscale hotel buildings, but keeps control of the branding of the hotels through franchise agreements.

Bass creates and launches a new hotel brand, Staybridge Suites by Holiday Inn. It's an entry into the profitable North American upscale extended stay market. Staybridge Suites becomes the fastest brand in this segment to reach 50 units in the Americas.

1998 Bass acquires the InterContinental hotel company, adding an upper upscale brand to its hotel portfolio. It's an acquisition that brings considerable synergies and cost savings.

2000 By acquiring Southern Pacific Hotels Corporation (SPHC) in Australia, Bass confirms its position as the leading hotel company in Asia Pacific.

It also acquires Bristol Hotels & Resorts Inc., a US-based hotel management company comprising 112 hotels operating mainly under leases. This gives the group a stronger management contract presence in the world's largest hotel market.

2000 The group sells Bass Brewers to a major Belgian brewer for £2.3 billion.

This marks the final step in refocusing the group from a domestic brewing operation to a leading international hospitality retailer—a process that has taken over ten years to complete.

It also involves the sale of the Bass name and a change of name to Six Continents PLC-a name that better reflects the global spread of the group's businesses.

2001 In February, Six Continents sells 988 smaller, unbranded pubs for £625 million.

In April, it acquires the European Posthouse chain of hotels for £810 million. The chain has hotels in strategic locations that are suitable for conversion to Holiday Inn, consolidating the Holiday Inn brand in the UK and Europe.

The group buys the InterContinental Hong Kong for £241 million, strengthening its position in the upscale hotel market in the key Chinese and Asia Pacific markets.

2002 On 1 October, Six Continents PLC announces the proposed separation of the group's hotels and soft drinks businesses (to be called InterContinental Hotels Group PLC) from the retail business (to be called Mitchells & Butlers PLC), and the return of £700 million of capital to shareholders.

This process is completed on 15 April 2003. InterContinental Hotels Group PLC (IHG) is now a distinct, discrete company, listed in the UK and the US stock markets.

2003 In July, IHG sells 16 Staybridge Suites hotels to Hospitality Properties Trust (HPT) and enters into a 20-year management agreement. In December, IHG adds the midscale extended-stay brand Candlewood Suites to its portfolio.

2004 In April, IHG announces the introduction of a new brand, Hotel Indigo, focused on providing affordable boutique accommodation. In the same month, the group adopts new standards for selling or re-selling hotel rooms for guest stays through online travel companies.

2005 Following the success of the extended-stay Staybridge Suites brand in North America, IHG launches Staybridge Suites UK in April 2005.

IHG announces the disposal of 100% of its holding in Britvic PLC. IHG is now a company with a pure hotels focus.

2006 IHG signs an operating joint venture with All Nippon Airways (ANA). The resulting joint venture—IHG ANA Hotels Group Japan—will be the largest international hotel operator in Japan, the world's second largest hotel market. The deal sees the introduction of three new brands created for Japan: ANA-InterContinental, ANA-Crowne Plaza and ANA-Holiday Inn.

2007 IHG announces a worldwide relaunch of the Holiday Inn brand family, comprising Holiday Inn, Express by Holiday Inn and Holiday Inn Express. The relaunch programme will give Holiday Inn a refreshed and contemporary brand image. All Holiday Inn hotels open or under development are expected to have implemented the relaunch programme by the end of 2010, with the first due to open in mid 2008 in the US.

(2) Philosophy—Winning Ways.

- Do the right thing
- Show we care
- Aim higher
- Show we celebrate differences
- Work better together

Company's core purpose—"Great Hotels Guests Love".

(3) Hotel brands (7). InterContinental Hotels & Resorts®, Crowne Plaza®, Hotel Indigo®, Holiday Inn®, Holiday Inn Express®, Staybridge Suites® and Candlewood Suites®.

InterContinental Hotels & Resorts is the most prestigious hotel brand, located in major cities in over 60 countries worldwide, offering business and leisure travellers the highest level of service and facilities.

57002 rooms, 168 hotels, 62 hotels in the pipeline

A dynamic hotel brand located in nearly 60 countries around the world. Truly international, Crowne Plaza offers premium accommodation, designed for the discerning business and leisure traveller who appreciates simplified elegance.

103678 rooms, 376 hotels, 125 hotels in the pipeline

A new innovative brand designed for the style-conscious traveller looking for the individual approach and facilities of a boutique hotel. Our hotels are located in urban, mid-town and suburban areas, close to businesses, restaurants and entertainment venues throughout America.

4264 rooms, 36 hotels, 57 hotels in the pipeline

Holiday Inn offers business and leisure travellers dependability, friendly service, modern facilities and excellent value. You'll find them throughout the world – in small towns and major cities, along quiet roadways and near bustling airports.

240025 rooms, 1315 hotels, 308 hotels in the pipeline

A fresh, clean, uncomplicated hotel choice offering comfort, convenience and good value. Holiday Inn Express (or Express by Holiday Inn) is one of the fastest growing hotel brands in its segment.

192264 rooms, 2101 hotels, 501 hotels in the pipeline

Staybridge Suites is an all-suite hotel brand for extended-stay guests looking for a residential-style hotel for business, relocation or leisure.

20323 rooms, 184 hotels, 110 hotels in the pipeline

Candlewood Suites' high-quality accommodation caters to mid-market business and leisure travellers looking for a multiple night hotel stay.

26996 rooms, 273 hotels, 139 hotels in the pipeline

3. Acccor Hotels & Resorts

(1) Hotel History. The world's leading hotel manager and market leader in Europe, Accor is unique in offering an extensive range of accommodations, from luxury to budget. It operates in nearly 90 countries with 4163 hotels and nearly 500000 rooms. Since the opening, in 1967, of the first Novotel in Lille Lesquin to today, a wonderful story has been written. It's the time it takes to go from one hotel to 4100, from one country to 90, from one employee to over 145000...

(2) Culture.

Core values:

- **Innovation** is our trademark.
- **The spirit of conquest** is our growth engine.
- **Performance** is the key to our continued success.
- **Respect** is basis of all our relationships.
- **Trust** is the foundation of our management.

Philosophy:

As guests of the Earth, we welcome the world.

(3) Brands. The Group's hotel operations include about **14 complementary brands—from luxury to budget**—that are recognized and appreciated around the world for their service quality: Sofitel, Pullman, MGallery, Novotel, Suite Novotel, Mercure, ibis, all seasons, Etap hotel, hotelF1, Motel6, as well as Thalassa sea & spa and Lenôtre. Accor's brands offer hotel stays tailored to the specific needs of each business and leisure customer.

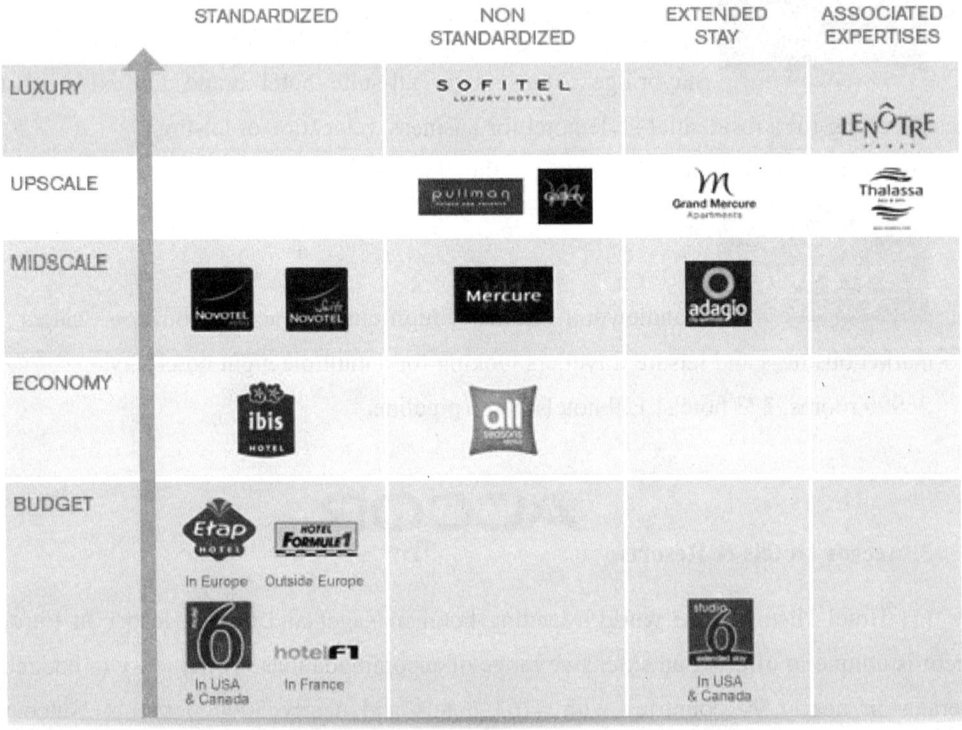

STANDARDIZED
NON STANDARDIZED
EXTENDED STAY
ASSOCIATED EXPERTISES
LUXURY
UPSCALE
MIDSCALE
ECONOMY
BUDGET
SOFITEL
LENÔTRE
pullman
Grand Mercure
Thalassa
NOVOTEL
Suite NOVOTEL
Mercure
adagio
ibis
all seasons
Etap HOTEL
HOTEL FORMULE 1
In Europe
Outside Europe
hotelF1
In USA & Canada
In France
studio 6
In USA & Canada

SOFITEL

LUXURY HOTELS **Life is Magnifique**

Sofitel offers luxury hotels in the world's most popular destinations and capitals, and combines French elegance, know-how and refinement with the best of the local culture. Focusing on interior design, tableware, service, consistency throughout the network, renovations, and other improvements, in 2009 the brand continued to raise its standards to satisfy its cosmopolitan clientele seeking unbeatable quality and excellence. And, from Rabat to Shanghai via Dubai, prestigious new establishments have joined the network.

pullman HOTELS AND RESORTS

"Check-in. Chill-out"

Pullman offers upscale hotels for business travelers in regional and international capitals around the world. Pullman hotels are conceived for welcoming and engaging hospitality, providing a complete array of personalized services and innovative technologies. Pullman has also introduced the groundbreaking "Co-Meeting" concept to ensure flawless success for meetings and events.

M Gallery

MGallery, "the art of staying"

MGallery is a new collection of upscale hotels, each with a marked personality. They will appeal to individual travelers looking for distinctive services or seeking a place with a true soul.

Whether located downtown or in prime tourist areas, each hotel in the collection offers an inimitable setting in which guests will enjoy a singular hotel experience reflecting a philosophy of pleasure.

m Grand Mercure

Superbly individual hotels and apartments

Situated in the Asia Pacific region, Grand Mercure is a network of properties renowned for their individuality and the quality of the guest experience. From ski chalets and historic country manor houses to spacious apartments in outstanding locations, Grand Mercure encompasses hotels and apartments in prime city and country locations. Each stands apart due to the space, quality and comfort offered—and each one is original, expressing the spirit of their region.

NOVOTEL HOTELS

Novotel, designed for natural living

Located in the main international destinations, Novotel promotes the wellbeing of business and leisure travellers, with spacious rooms equipped for work and relaxation, a 24/24 healthy-eating restaurant service, meeting rooms, attentive staff, special children's areas and fitness and relaxation facilities.

Suite Novotel nurtures an off-beat, avant-garde spirit that invites guests to experience a new way of hotel living. Targeting a medium-stay clientele, Suite Novotel offers 30m² Suites which are fully flexible so the guest can arrange the space to suit his or her needs (sleep, relaxation, work). For Suite Novotel's frequent traveler clientele, round-the-clock services promise more freedom and autonomy for a truly pleasurable stay.

For more than 35 years, Mercure has exemplified expert hospitality and personalized service. Operating in nearly 50 countries around the world, Mercure boasts hotels with distinctive personalities carefully preserved through the type of services offered and the decor, both of which vary from one hotel to the next. In the heart of the city, in the mountains, by the sea or in the countryside, each Mercure hotel has an authentic style.

The city at your own rhythm

Enjoy some of Europe's largest cities at your own rhythm thanks to an innovative accommodation concept for all your medium and long stays. Ready to live in apartments with à la carte hotel services and degressive rates according to your length of stay (4 nights and more).

Hotels, the way you like them

ibis, the worldwide economy hotel brand of the Accor group, offers consistent quality accommodation and services in all its hotels, for the best local value: a well-designed and fully-equipped en-suite bedroom, major hotel services available 24/7 and a wide choice of on-site food and beverage options.

all seasons HOTELS

Is all you need

The hotel where the little extras don't cost extra! A new non-standardized economy brand for anyone looking to "consume better," all seasons offers all-inclusive hotels that combine simplicity and generosity, quality, conviviality and proximity.

Whether located downtown or in another leading activity center, each all seasons hotel has its own personality while sharing the same bright, colorful spirit of a brand full of energy with a good dose of humor.

Etap HOTEL

Be smart. Stay smart.

European leader in budget hotels with more than 400 hotels in 15 countries, Etap Hotel offers to its guests, at affordable rates, comfortable rooms for one to three people, WiFi Internet access, all-you-can-eat breakfast buffet, snacks and beverages products, and « great deals » available year round at etaphotel.com. The same product is present in the Southern Hemisphere with the Formule1 brand.

hotelF1

Pay less travel more

Created in 1984, Formule1 revolutionized the world of hotellery in Europe proposing a comfortable room for one, two or three persons. Became the reference of "low cost" hotels, Formule1 keep going and becomes hotelF1 in France.

motel 6

"We'll Leave the Light on For You.®"*

North American chain of budget motels in North America

Established in 1962 in Santa Barbara, California, Motel6 is a leader in budget hotels in the United States and is also present in Canada. The chain offers its clients many services: cable television with premium channels like HBO and ESPN, free local calls, free coffee in the morning, non smoking rooms, free accommodation for children and WiFi Internet connection at most locations—all at the lowest price of any American hotel chain. Motel6 guarantees the best price value at all of its locations.

studio 6 extended stay

"Extend Your Stay, not Your Budget"*

North American chain of extended-stay hotels in North America

Studio6 extended stay hotels offer the affordable comfort of furnished studios, low weekly rates and accommodating hotel amenities. Travelers will find Studio6 in the United States and Canada conveniently located in major business complexes, offering easy access to shopping and retail centers, entertainment areas, and restaurants.

Thalassa SEA & SPA

Thalassa sea & spa, taking you to places your body will never forget.

At sites pre-selected for their outstanding beauty, experts from the Thalassa sea & spa network invite you to discover all the benefits of sea-water, rich in mineral salts and trace elements and indispensable to the organism. And the virtues of hot spring water and each and every spa-related therapy.

LENÔTRE PARIS

Creator of upscale gourmet dining

A prestigious signature of the Accor Group, Lenôtre is an ambassador for French gastronomy throughout the world. Pastries and cakes, catering, chocolates, candies, reception planning, restaurants—Lenôtre comprises 45 luxury gastronomy establishments in

9 countries, and is pursuing its strategic development, notably in the Middle East and south-east Asia. A partner to major international events, a prestigious caterer, member of the Comité Colbert, Lenôtre serves the top-rated tables at the Pré Catelan and the Pavillon Elysée Lenôtre restaurants. Lenôtre cooking and pastry schools are attended by professionals and a growing number of amateur gastronomy practitioners.

4. Hilton Worldwide

(1) History. Hilton Worldwide offers business and leisure travelers the finest in accommodations, service, amenities and value. Since Conrad Hilton bought his first hotel in 1919 in Cisco, Texas, it has expanded geographically, produced original hotel and travel concepts, and developed innovative technologies to enhance the guest experience. Today Hilton Worldwide is the leading global hospitality company, spanning the lodging sector from luxurious full-service hotels and resorts to extended-stay suites and mid-priced hotels.

(2) Culture.

Vision: To fill the earth with the light and warmth of hospitality.

Mission: We will be the preeminent global hospitality company—the first choice of guests, team members and owners alike.

Values:

H HOSPITALITY—We are passionate about delivering exceptional guest experiences.

I INTEGRITY—We do the right thing, all the time.

L LEADERSHIP—We are leaders in our industry and in our communities.

T TEAMWORK—We are team players in everything we do.

O OWNERSHIP—We are the owners of our actions and decisions.

N NOW—We operate with a sense of urgency and discipline.

(3) Brands. Hilton Worldwide presents guests with ten leading hotel brands and more than 3600 hotels in 81 countries, with luxurious full-service hotels and resorts to comfortable extended stay suites, quality mid price hotels and relaxing vacation ownership properties. The brands include Waldorf Astoria Hotels & Resorts, Conrad Hotels & Resorts, Hilton Hotels & Resorts, Doubletree, Embassy Suites Hotels, Hilton Garden Inn, Hampton Inn & Suites, Homewood Suites by Hilton, Home2 Suites by Hilton and Hilton Grand Vacations. All the brands participate in the world-class frequent-guest program Hilton HHonors.

Loyalty Program

HHONORS
HILTON WORLDWIDE

Luxury

WALDORF ASTORIA HOTELS & RESORTS

CONRAD HOTELS & RESORTS

Full Service

Hilton HOTELS & RESORTS

DOUBLETREE

EMBASSY SUITES HOTELS

Focused Service

Hilton Garden Inn

Hampton

HOMEWOOD SUITES Hilton

HOME2 SUITES BY HILTON

Timeshare

Hilton Grand Vacations

5. Starwood Hotels and Resorts

(1) History.

1991 Starwood Capital Partners, a real estate acquisition company backed by high net worth families, is formed in Chicago.

1993 Starwood Capital buys its first hotels, and by 1994 owns interests in more than 30 properties.

1995 Starwood Capital acquires the debt of a distressed NYSE listed company call

Hotel Investors Trust, "a paired share" REIT, and renames it Starwood Lodging. Starwood stock rises 72.46% on the year!

1997 In September, Starwood Lodging announces an agreement to purchase Westin Hotels & Resorts for $1.8 billion. The following month Starwood Lodging announces an agreement to purchase ITT Sheraton Corporation for $14.3 billion, acting as a white knight against a hostile bid from Hilton. Starwood is set to become a global enterprise. Starwood stock ends the year up by 57.48%.

1998 In January, Starwood Lodging completes the acquisition of Westin Hotels & Resorts. With the completion of the purchase, Starwood Lodging is renamed Starwood Hotels & Resorts. In February, Starwood completes the acquisition of ITT Sheraton Corporation. Starwood's portfolio now includes more than 650 hotels and resorts in more than 70 countries worldwide.

The first W Hotel opens in December in New York City. The W brand is designed to offer the personality and individuality of an independent, one-of-a-kind hotel, while guaranteeing the reliability and superior level of amenities and services business travelers require. W features casually elegant guest rooms and a hip, urban style.

1999 Starwood acquires Vistana, Inc., a vacation ownership company, to establish an immediate presence in the growing vacation ownership market. It later becomes Starwood Vacation Ownership, one of the most profitable segments of the company. Starwood launches Starwood Preferred Guest® to aggressively reward and recognize frequent travelers. The program makes headlines with its policy of no blackout dates and no capacity controls—both industry firsts!

Westin introduces the Heavenly Bed®, featuring a pillow-top mattress, down comforter and luxurious, all white bed linens. It is an immediate success.

The St. Regis brand grows from one hotel in New York City to six hotels all named to *Condé Nast Traveler's* "Gold" list for 1999!

Four Points by Sheraton opens its 100th hotel, the Four Points by Sheraton Santa Monica in California.

2001 Starwood Hotels & Resorts Worldwide, Inc. is named the World's Leading Hotel Group at the Eight Annual World Travel Awards!

Starwood Preferred Guest is voted Program of the Year for the second consecutive year during the 13th Annual Freddie Awards (since renamed the Frequent Traveler Awards), one of the most prestigious honors in the travel industry.

Westin introduces the Heavenly Bath® in North American hotels, offering guests a temptation to leave the Heavenly Bed in the morning. Starwood introduces the Westin

Heavenly Crib® and the Sheraton and Four Points by Sheraton Sweet Sleeper Crib in North America.

2003 Starwood announces that its Sheraton, Westin, and W hotels will welcome dogs in the U.S. and Canada. As part of the Starwood LTD (Love That Dog) program, four-legged guests will receive luxurious dog beds and amenities like plush robes, doggie toys, and canine massages.

Sheraton Hotels & Resorts introduces the Sheraton Sweet Sleeper™ Bed, featuring an 11.5-inch thick high coil count Sealy Posturepedic Plush Top mattress, down and allergy sensitive pillows, and crisp cotton sheets. This is the latest in a series of enhancements designed to elevate the brand to the top of the upscale hotel segment.

2005 For the sixth year in a row, Starwood Preferred Guest is voted Program of the Year in both America and internationally during the 17th Annual Freddie Awards. Starwood Preferred Guest continues its success as one of the most well-respected programs in the industry.

2006 Starwood acquires Le Méridien, a brand created to share and extend the international experience. 137 properties, primarily located in Europe and the Middle East, become part of the Starwood family.

2007 Starwood announces its much-anticipated new brands in the select-service hotel category: Aloft Hotels and Element Hotels. Conceived by the team that created W Hotels, Aloft Hotels will raise the bar in the select-service category, offering urban-inspired, loft-like guest rooms, enhanced technology services, landscaped outdoor spaces for socializing day and night, and an energetic lounge scene. Inspired by Westin Hotels & Resorts, Element Hotels intends to promote balance through flowing, multi-purpose spaces with an emphasis on environmentally-friendly design.

2008 The first Aloft and Element hotels open in Lexington, Massachusetts.

2009 Starwood invests $6 billion in enhancements as part of the Sheraton Revitalization project. 60 new and 120 newly renovated Sheraton Hotels & Resorts around the world benefit from the revitalization effort which includes 300 new lobbies, 70000 new guest rooms, 100000 new beds and the brand's unique wired lobby lounge, the Link@Sheraton℠ experienced with Microsoft®.

2010 Starwood celebrates a significant milestone with the opening of its 1000th hotel! The Sheraton Qiandao Lake Resort opens on the shores of China's famed Qiandao Lake.

(2) Philosophy.

① Mission and values. At Starwood, our mission and values are the core of how we do business. We believe in genuine collaboration, fostering trust and respect, and re-imagining our business through creativity and innovation. We believe our values make Starwood a great place to work.

② Our service culture. We believe in our service culture—it is not about what we do but how we do it. Our commitment to customer satisfaction is one of Starwood's key differentiators, and is what makes the difference between a good company and a great one.

③ Diversity & inclusion: We believe diversity and inclusion are not just nice things to talk about, but a business imperative. Our success is dependent on a variety of talents, opinions, and backgrounds and we constantly strive to improve in this area.

④ Community partnerships: We believe we are part of a global community and place great value on our community partnerships. We know that a great company is one that has a positive impact on the world around us.

⑤ Company values: Go the Extra Step by taking actions that build lasting connections and loyalty, Play as a Team by working globally and across all teams in the company; Do the Right Thing by using good judgment, respecting our communities, associates, owners, partners and the environment.

(3) Brands. The brands include: Le Méridien®, Element℠ Hotels, Aloft℠ Hotels, Sheraton® Hotels & Resorts, The Luxury Collection®, St. Regis® Hotels & Resorts, Westin® Hotels & Resorts, W Hotels® and Four Points® by Sheraton.

As the largest of the Starwood Hotels & Resorts brands, **Sheraton** serves the needs of both business and leisure travelers in locations from Argentina to Zimbabwe. Encouraged to call upon their own experiences to put their guests at ease, Sheraton associates connect with them in a personal way.

Four Points by Sheraton offers guests a comfortable visit at the right price in a room well-equipped with business and personal amenities. Associates at Four Points by Sheraton delight self-sufficient travelers with a new kind of comfort, approachable style, and can-do service. They strive to uncomplicate their guests' day and provide them with a delightful, relaxing experience.

Warm, wonderful, witty, wired...welcome. With a perfect balance of style and substance, **W Hotels** redefines and reinvents the upscale hotel experience. The talent at W Hotels is invited to meet and exceed the guest's expectations in unexpected and unique ways. They are inviting, flirty, refreshing and thoughtful and they wow the guest in a playful environment, showing them an insider's view.

Say aloha to the new twist on travel... **aloft hotels** is a new destination sensation offering a sassy * refreshing * oasis in the travel desert. **aloft hotels** talent take a fresh, energetic approach to everything in life...and they know how to juggle without dropping anything. Always with a playful personality but never without substance, aloft talent effortlessly deliver style, ease and a refreshing retreat from the road.

The Luxury Collection is a group of unique hotels and resorts offering exceptional service to an elite clientele. All of these hotels, some of them centuries old, are internationally recognized as being among the world's finest. The Luxury Collection hotels and resorts are distinguished by magnificent décor, spectacular settings, impeccable service and the latest in modern conveniences and amenities. Staff members at Luxury Collection hotels and resorts are given the authority to far exceed the expectations of a very discerning clientele.

Le Méridien offers a unique European experience with a French flair in the world's top destinations throughout Europe, the Americas, Asia Pacific, the Middle East and Africa. Friendly and outgoing, Le Méridien associates proudly strive to make each and every guest experience pleasant and positive. They are always prepared to put in the extra effort that makes the difference between expected and outstanding service.

Inspired by Westin, **element** is a wholly different hotel combining modern design, smart thinking, clever use of space and upscale amenities for extended stay travelers. Decidedly modern, element is intuitively designed with clean, smart use of the space that encourages guests' productivity and sense of being in control. Associates at element have a mission. Empowered to innovate, they are encouraged to find ways that help guests realize their true potential. Respected, honored, and dedicated, they are an integral part of element's goal of creating an environment that inspires rejuvenation.

Westin Hotels & Resorts redefines efficient service with an effortless style and gracious attitude that ensures a truly unforgettable experience. Every Westin is a haven of serenity and a distinctive alternative for those who appreciate a higher standard. Supported by sumptuous amenities such as the Heavenly Bed® and Heavenly Bath®, Westin associates are empowered to "de-stress" their guests and serve them on the "road to renewal".

Only a select few of the world's luxury hotels merit the reputation of offering unprecedented excellence in standards of hospitality and elegance. Of those, there is the top tier: **St. Regis Hotels & Resorts**. St. Regis offers a unique refuge of timeless elegance, unwavering taste, and unrivaled care and courtesy that simply cannot be found elsewhere. The impeccable staff takes pride in far exceeding the performance of customary duties and has the authority to go to any lengths to ensure the utmost in comfort, down to the minutest detail.

Appendix C

Listening Script

Interview One

1.

Interviewer: Good afternoon. Please, have a seat.

Applicant: Good afternoon. Thank you.

2.

Interviewer: To begin, could you please tell me a little something about yourself?

Applicant: My name is Jessie. I'm from Jinan, Shandong Province. I've been studying at the Shandong College of Tourism and Hospitality for two years now, majoring in Hotel Management. I like to keep busy and stay in shape. I live an active lifestyle, always finding the time to get exercise before or after my classes, and enjoy reading to relax in my spare time.

3.

Interviewer: Please tell me something about your work experience.

Applicant: I worked as a waitress at a 5-star hotel in Beijing over the last summer holiday. It was a great experience as I was able to develop the skills that I learned at my school, such as setting tables, taking orders, delivering the food and drinks to the tables as well as dealing with the bill and handling cash and credit cards. I also learned how to work under pressure and as part of a team in a busy restaurant environment.

4.

Interviewer: Describe a situation in which you were successful.

Applicant: One day I was working in the hotel's restaurant, and a large party arrived. I had only worked with smaller groups of customers before, so I was a bit concerned. But, after telling myself that if I relaxed and kept focused, I could easily handle such a large number of guests. In the end, I provided them with excellent service, and they seemed to have really enjoyed their meal.

5.

Interviewer: Why should I hire you?

Applicant: After working this summer I have practical experience in F&B. I want to learn as much as I can about different departments so I have an understanding of how they work together to make the hotel run smoothly. I'm a quick learner, a hard worker and I'm always willing to ask for advice if I'm not sure how to handle a new situation.

6.

Interviewer: Is there anything you'd like to ask about our hotel?

Applicant: Yes, please. I'd like to know if the hotel promotes from within the organization rather than hiring from the outside.

Interviewer: Yes, we certainly do promote our staff based on performance evaluations. We have employees that started in entry-level positions that have gone on to manage Food and Beverage outlets.

Applicant: Thank you.

7.

Interviewer: Thank you for your time. We'll be in contact within two to three weeks. Goodbye.

Applicant: Thank you very much. Goodbye.

Interview Two

1.

Interviewer: Good morning. Have a seat, please.

Applicant: Good morning. Thank you.

2.

Interviewer: Please, tell me something about yourself.

Applicant: My name is Jessie. I major in Food and Beverage and enjoy learning new things about this field. I'm a part of the school's Student Union and help to organize and put on school events. I like playing badminton and jogging. So, with those activities and my studies my days are quite busy.

3.

Interviewer: Why did you choose to major in Food and Beverage?

Applicant: I've always enjoyed helping my mother prepare and serve food at home, especially when we had guests over the holidays. I think being a waitress is the perfect job for me because I like dealing with people. And, you get to see the results right away when you've done a good job. The customers leave satisfied with the good service you provided.

4.

Interviewer: Tell me about your career goals.

Applicant: My biggest goal is to get into a management position. But first, I want to learn as much as I can about the hotel industry, from the ground up. I think that managers should know as much as they can about each department and how they work together in order to understand the needs of any department.

5.

Interviewer: How long do you plan to stay with our hotel?

Applicant: Working for your hotel meets my career goals. As long as you are happy with my work, and I'm happy in my work for you, I expect to stay there as long as possible.

6.

Applicant: Pardon me. May I ask a question?

Interviewer: Of course.

Applicant: How do you evaluate an employee's performance and how often?

Interviewer: During your six-month probation period, you will have a body trainer responsible for training you regarding the hotel's standards. The body trainer is responsible for you and reports to the manager, who will evaluate you once or twice a month during this time. After six months you will receive a manager appraisal through HR Dept. If the manager's assessment is positive, your probation will end and you'll be officially part of the team. After that, you will be evaluated once a year.

Applicant: Thank you. That's very helpful.

7.

Interviewer: Thank you for your time. We'll let you know the results in a few weeks.

Applicant: Thank you. Goodbye.

Interview Three

1.

Interviewer: Good morning. Please, have a seat.

Applicant: Good morning. Thank you.

2.

Interviewer: Besides what's written in your resume, is there anything else you can tell me about yourself?

Applicant: My boy friend has been working with your hotel group for years, from whom I've learned a lot about your hotel. Actually I admire him for working in such a nice hotel. He also hopes that I can join him in your hotel.

3.

Interviewer: Why did you choose to attend the Shandong College of Tourism and Hospitality?

Applicant: I think that the fact that tourism is growing so rapidly in China today made me feel a sense of excitement about the opportunities a career in a the Hospitality industry. I also knew that this school could help me develop skills that I could use anywhere in the world.

4.

Interviewer: What's your greatest strength?

Applicant: I'd have to say that I'm a hard worker. Both with my studies at school or when I've had a job, I always apply myself to my work with all of my heart. When I'm faced with a difficult problem, I always believe that if I make the effort and give it all of my energy, I can solve it.

5.

Interviewer: How do you usually deal with criticism?

Applicant: I appreciate constructive criticism because it will help me to do my job better. I don't have a problem with criticism since I always try to communicate with my supervisor and coworkers so that I can deal with any problems before they get to the point where criticism is necessary.

6.

Interviewer: Why do you want to work for us?

Applicant: At our school I've heard a lot about your hotel, and know that you provide excellent service to your guests. With my education and training so far, I believe that I can be an asset to your team, helping to continue the organization to provide the best service to your customers.

7.

Interviewer: Thanks for your time. We'll let you know our decision within a few weeks.

Applicant: Thank you. Goodbye.

Interview Four

1.

Interviewer: Good morning. Please, have a seat.

Applicant: Good morning. Thank you.

2.

Interviewer: Could you tell me something about your personality?

Applicant: I am easy-going. I know that everyone is different, but I am always ready to find others' merits, which helps me a lot in life.

3.

Interviewer: Do you have any work experience?

Applicant: I worked in the Four Star Hotel in Beijing over the summer in the Housekeeping Department. My duties included cleaning guestrooms, changing the linens and restocking the toiletries and mini-bars.

4.

Interviewer: How have your education and training prepared you for this job?

Applicant: My education gave me the knowledge that I'll need to be successful. My training taught me how to use what I'd learned properly. Before my training, I was pretty sure I could do the job well. The training allowed me to use my education and gave me confidence that I could face future challenges and succeed.

5.

Interviewer: Do you prefer to work with other people, or alone?

Applicant: Teamwork is very important in the hotel industry. If you can't work well as a part of a team, you probably don't communicate well with other people. Working as a team is important, but if I have to, I can work just as well alone. I like the challenge of dealing with situations by myself and don't always need direction. Tell me what needs to be done and I'll find a way to do it.

6.

Interviewer: What is your greatest weakness?

Applicant: I think that sometimes I'm a little impatient. My friends have pointed this out to me. Now that I realize it, I work hard to not let it get in the way of relationships at school or at work. I've learned to tell when I'm losing my patience and remind myself that sometimes you have to wait to get the best results.

7.

Interviewer: Thank you for coming. We'll get in touch with the results in two to three week's time.

Applicant: Thank you. Goodbye.

Interview Five

1.

Interviewer: Good afternoon. Please, have a seat.

Applicant: Good morning. Thank you.

2.

Interviewer: Please, tell me about yourself.

Applicant: My name is _______. I major in Western Cuisine and have been studying here for a year and a half now. My father and mother run a small restaurant in my home town and I help them when I'm back home on holidays, so I know a lot about Chinese cooking, but I want to continue to develop my skills in Western Cuisine.

3.

Interviewer: Tell me something that you would like to improve about yourself.

Applicant: At school I've studied Western dining and cuisine, but I would like to learn as much as possible about Western style service. I look for all of the information I can on the Internet in my spare time, since it's important knowledge to have to work in many countries around the world.

4.

Interviewer: How do you work under pressure?

Applicant: One thing I've learned both in school and during my time working over the last holiday, is that communication helps a lot when it comes to dealing with pressure and stress. I think it's better to ask someone for help instead of letting a problem get out of control. Also, if I feel pressure at work, I remind myself that getting some exercise after work will help me get a good night's sleep so I'll be ready to go back feeling refreshed and relaxed.

5.

Interviewer: How do you feel about working overtime?

Applicant: From my experience working in my family restaurant, I know that sometimes there are more guests and more work to be done. Sometimes you don't have time to rest during mealtimes, but I've learned how to pace myself so that I can get the job done. I realize that a restaurant or hotel is only as strong as its workforce, so I'm willing to make an extra effort to help the organization provide the best service possible.

6.

Interviewer: Do you have any questions you'd like to ask about this position or our organization?

Applicant: Yes, please. How long to employees generally stay with your hotel?

Interviewer: We've got employees from China, even from your school who've been with us for four years or more and they've been able to move into higher level positions as a result of their hard work and commitment.

Applicant: Thank you.

7.

Interviewer: Thank you for coming. We'll let you know the results within a few weeks. Goodbye.

Applicant: Thank you. Goodbye.

Appendix D

部分章节翻译

第1章　面试标准

面试官期待从应试者那里得到什么？不同的酒店和酒店集团对应试人员有不同的标准。然而，我们仍然能够从中找到它们的相同之处。

对于一个希望在国内外品牌酒店找到工作的应试者来说，他所关心的首要问题是酒店对应试者的要求或面试标准。毕竟，只有知道了标准或面试官的期待才能知道该做什么准备，以便达到酒店的需求并且面试成功。而且，当得知面试官的期待之后，你的准备才可能充分。

研究某些品牌酒店集团面试应试者的评价标准是有益的，这有助于应试者对此问题有清晰的了解。

以下是5份国际知名酒店在中国招聘时的评价表。

……

总之，求职面试者应在以下方面做好准备：

- 仪容仪表
- 口头交流
- 个人性格
- 职业能力

1.1　仪容仪表

首先，应试者给潜在雇主的第一印象是至关重要的。面试官的第一眼就落在应试者的形象上。因此，职业化整洁的打扮和恰当的服装就像是递给面试官的名片一样，.而面试官最初的评判就是基于应试者的相貌和服装做出的。这就是为什么求职面试着职业装始终至关重要的缘由。

……

1.2 口头交流

使用外语表述是一个挑战。然而，切记语言是交流的工具。面试官要弄明白的是，在面试过程中应试者是否能用外语表述自己的思想，是否能够避免由于遣词用句不当，甚至语塞而造成误解或中断的现象。简明而有逻辑性的表述意味着对语言的精通和思维的清晰。基于语言能力的相互交流应该列为应试者的首要能力。

除了词汇和语法，语音和语调也是影响口头交流的因素。总体上来说，蹩脚的语音语调尽管不像用词造句出现的错误带来那么严重的后果，但是，仍然会给面试官对应试者的评价带来负面的影响。毕竟，评价一个其母语不是英语的面试者的英语表达能力是面试官必须考虑的项目之一。

总之，自然流畅的口头交流，简明而富有逻辑性的表述，清晰、生动而富有韵律的声音是口语交流能力的佐证。

1.3 个人性格

应试者的个人性格是面试官关注的另一个方面。面试官期待应试者的品格、性情以及心理特质均能符合酒店对从业人员的要求。

其个性特征，如细腻、耐心、乐观、开朗、乐于助人、热情、自信、有合作意识、有创新精神等，不仅在社交中令人愉快，而且在职业上也颇受欢迎，因为酒店向顾客销售的是服务。无疑，这种服务是带有从业者个人的性格和行为特征的。

1.4 职业能力

职业能力即工作的能力。酒店从业人员的能力是建立在从业者所受的教育和积累的工作经验之上的。能力使一个人在岗位上履行其职责成为可能。从教育和工作经验中，从业者获得其岗位所必需的知识、技能。因此，对于一个面试官来说，能力……

第3章 面试问题分类及分析

前言

面试是一项精心策划的活动，对于面试官和面试者来说，都需要进行充分的思考和周密的计划。中国古语云：知己知彼，百战不殆。为了最终通过面试获得工作机会，面试者应该熟悉可能遇到的面试问题、问题背后的动机以及如何恰当地回答。本章划分为 3 个部分，分别讨论上述问题。

3.1 面试问题分类

1. 以顾客为中心的问题

(1) 你认为我们的顾客期待什么样的服务？

(2) 你如何判断一位顾客满意与否？顾客若不满意，你会采取哪些步骤解决这个问题？

(3) 如果顾客邀请你去夜店，你会怎么做？

(4) 告诉我你曾经独自应对难缠顾客的经历。

(5) 你曾经如何应对难缠的顾客？

(6) 描述一下你理想的工作。

2. 有关团队的问题

(1) 描述一个你最近参与过的团队或小组。

(2) 描述一下你在团队中所起的作用。

(3) 当团队其他成员积极配合你的时候，你觉得你的行为效力有多大？当他们消极应对呢？

(4) 你的同事如何描述你？

(5) 其他人怎么表扬你的？在顾客、同事、老板、下属眼中，你的缺点是什么？

(6) 你与来自哪些国家的人共过事？

(7) 当一位同事需要帮助的时候，描述一下他需要什么，在哪里，什么时候，你是如何帮助他的。举例说明。

(8) 你具有良好的团队合作精神吗？为什么？

3. 有关个人能力的问题

(1) 关于规划日常事务，你有哪些经验？

(2) 你认为组织完成一个项目的关键步骤是什么？

(3) 举例说明你是如何对自己的学习负责的。

(4) 什么样的培训需求能帮助你提升职业生涯？

(5) 你在工作中有什么不足？

(6) 你从个人错误中收获了什么？

(7) 什么事情能给你灵感？

(8) 去年你是如何提升自己的？

(9) 你能胜任独立工作吗？

(10) 如果我告诉你我不喜欢你，你将如何改变我的想法？

(11) 你认为该工作需要哪些素质？
(12) 你在哪些方面比其他面试者略胜一筹？
(13) 你能胜任重压下的工作吗？

4. 关于执行力的问题

(1) 你如何确定一天之中各项事情的轻重缓急？
(2) 是什么驱使你来参加这次面试的？
(3) 你如何确保各项标准在酒店中得以实施？
(4) 质量是酒店行业的首要标准。你如何保证高质量？

5. 有关人员管理的问题

(1) 你在工作中的哪些方面需要与其他人合作？
(2) 举例说明，在职场上、大学里或家里，你必须解决的一个问题及如何解决的。
(3) 面对工作中出现的争论，一个人应该做什么？
(4) 为了使你所在城市的意大利餐厅在接下来的 3 个月里销售额实现增长，并具备潜在的市场，你会提供哪些建议？
(5) 你申请该职位是出于什么动机？
(6) 你能为我们单位贡献什么？

6. 有关教育背景及工作经验的问题

(1) 你在学校所学专业与此工作有何联系？
(2) 你从暑假兼职中收获了什么？
(3) 说出 3 件你从学校学到的而且可以应用于该工作的事情。
(4) 你如何评价你的学校、老师和同学？
(5) 学校里的什么事情使你最兴奋？

7. 常见问题

(1) 你希望从用人单位获得什么？
(2) 关于我们公司/酒店你了解什么？
(3) 你期待获得什么样的报酬？
(4) 为什么你认为你适合这份工作？
(5) 5 年之后的你会是什么样子？请说说你的 5 年计划。
(6) 你为什么申请了酒店的这个岗位？
(7) 能说一下这份工作的岗位职责吗？

3.2　面试官发问的动机

面试官总是期待在有限的时间里尽可能多地了解面试者，以便决定他/她是否是酒店的合适人选。因此，面试是对面试者的一项综合测评。作为目标明确的一项活动，面试是精心组织的，这意味着面试官绝不会随便发问，而是有着明确的动机和目标。鉴于此，面试者除了准备简历、独一无二的自我介绍、有可能被问到的问题外，最重要的是知晓面试官的动机。下面的部分将以典型例子作为辅助，分析面试官的提问动机。

(1) 典型问题：请说说你的家庭。

这是一个非常有代表性的问题。面试官并不想知道你的家乡在哪里或你的父母是做什么的，他真正想了解的是家庭环境对你的影响。回答问题时要围绕父母如何潜移默化地培养了你的个性和性格。类似的问题如下所示。

① 你喜欢什么样的个性特点？

② 你喜欢与什么样的人交朋友？

③ 你期待与什么样的同事共事？

④ 朋友和同学如何描述你？

⑤ 同事如何描述你？

⑥ 如何你是动物，你选择成为哪种动物？为什么？

……

这类问题背后隐含的动机是从家庭、朋友或你对他人的期待那里了解你的个性特点，以决定你是否适合这份工作。因此，回答问题时，应回答出工作岗位需要的性格特点，不要漫谈以致跑题。

参考回答：我家里有三口人，父母和我。父亲是高中语文教师，常年忙碌，他总是希望我能自理，独立做选择。母亲善良诚实，与邻为善，待人真诚。

(2) 典型问题：课余时间你常做些什么？

通过这个问题，面试官可以了解你的课外生活，但此处真正的动机是考查你的英语表达能力和仪容：你是否可以自如地应对日常话题，交流时是否有眼神交流，能否始终面带微笑，并恰当地使用肢体语言。另外，务必使你的回答清晰有逻辑。

参考回答：课余时间，我常常与朋友打羽毛球，读英文小说，例如《简·爱》、《远大前程》等，或是爬山。对我来说，课余时间很有必要，我希望可以充分利用课余时间来丰富头脑、强健身体。

类似的问题如下所示。

① 描述一个你最近参与过的团队或小组。

② 描述一下你在团队中所起的作用。

③ 你从错误中收获了什么？

④ 请说说你犯过的最严重的错误。

⑤ 请说一下曾经令你感动的一次经历或犯错误的一次经历。

⑥ 你喜欢什么类型的书籍、杂志或电视节目？

……

(3) 典型问题：你从暑假兼职中收获了什么？

面试官试图了解你的工作经历，这对你申请的职位或许是必要的。因此要确保你的回答正是面试官期待的。此外，准备好回答追击性问题，此类问题很容易被问到追击性问题。例如：

你在哪里兼职过？工作了多久？担任过什么岗位？你从中得到的最大收获是什么？你遇到过难缠的顾客吗？你是如何处理的？你的同事、主管或老板怎样描述你？……

例如，你申请的是服务生，对于这一岗位来说服务意识和责任心是必需的素质。回答上述问题时就应该围绕服务生这一岗位的要求展开。

参考回答：暑假里，我在济南的一家三星级酒店工作了一个多月，在此期间最大的收获是服务意识和责任感的提升。从顾客进入酒店直到他们离开，我都应该给予悉心关注，提供满意的服务。

类似的问题如下所示。

① 你认为顾客期待什么样的服务？

② 请描述一下你的岗位职责。

③ 请描述一下你理想的工作。

④ 你认为你工作中有难度的或有挑战性的部分是什么？

⑤ 你曾为酒店提供过哪些建议？

⑥ 请作一下工作职责描述。

……

(4) 典型问题：你为什么选择我们酒店而不是迪拜的其他酒店？

问此问题的动机是了解你申请该岗位的动机和期待。面试官最期待的回答是你可以为酒店做什么而不是酒店能带给你什么。去迪拜或许你可以提高英语，交到外国朋友，但这些都不是最重要的。

不要问酒店可以给你带来什么。

告诉面试官你能为酒店做什么。

图 3.1

参考回答：贵酒店具有开拓精神和开放性，在酒店业起到带头作用。贵酒店管理一流，且不断进步。我相信凭借我的能力和才干一定会为贵酒店作出一些贡献。

类似的问题如下所示。

① 是什么驱使你来参加这次面试的？

② 你为什么申请我们酒店的这个岗位？

③ 关于我们酒店，你了解什么？

④ 你最喜欢的工作是什么？

⑤ 你最喜欢什么样的领导？

⑥ 你喜欢什么样的公司或酒店？为什么？

⑦ 找工作时，你最先考虑的是哪个因素？

⑧ 你可以为我方酒店贡献什么？

……

(5) 典型问题：5 年之后的你将是什么样子？请说说你的 5 年计划。

关于职业生涯，你或许制定了 5 年计划甚至是更长远的计划，也或许没有任何职业规划，要是这样，你最好拿出时间认真规划一番。无论如何此类问题是有关你的抱负、自信心和进取心的。回答问题时恰当描述你的抱负、自信心和进取心。不要表现得太自大。

参考回答：我想通过良好的专业技能、勤奋的工作和令人满意的表现，在 5 年之后成为餐饮部的一名主管。

同时，准备好回答追击性问题，例如，你将如何实现这一计划或将其变为现实？

类似的问题如下所示。

① 去年你是如何提升自己的？

② 职业生涯中你毕生的梦想是什么？

③ 你认为可以通过本次面试吗？理由是什么？

④ 如果老板交给你非常难办的任务，你会怎么做？

⑤ 关于职业生涯你有什么规划吗？你将如何实现它？

……

(6) 典型问题：关于晚上或周末加班，你的观点是什么？

提问该问题的动机是了解你的工作态度、自律性和对工作的忠诚度。酒店更愿意选择那些遵守酒店规定、对酒店忠诚、对工作持有积极态度的员工。

参考回答：对我而言，如果酒店有急需，我一定加班。同时我也相信酒店会合理安排工作时间，把工作效率放在首位。

类似的问题如下所示。

① 如果顾客邀请你去夜店，你会怎么做？

② 你总是努力提升你的工作效率吗？用何种方式？

③ 你曾经给学校或工作过的酒店提出过合理化的建议吗？请举例说明。

④ 你期待在我方酒店工作多少年？

……

(7) 典型问题：你认为成功的关键是什么？为什么？

这个问题旨在考查你的分析和判断能力。作为酒店员工，你应该能够分析顾客需求、工作中的困难情况，并找到相应的解决方案。因此，要全面提升自己，做好求职准备。

参考回答：我认为成功的关键是精心的准备。没有人在没有准备的情况下就会成功。成功不会不请自来，我们必须做好充分的准备，努力做好该做的，抓住机会取得成功。

类似的问题如下所示。

① 你认为顾客期待什么样的服务？

② 你如何判断一位顾客满意与否？顾客若不满意，你会采取哪些步骤解决这个问题？

③ 你认为组织完成一项任务最重要的步骤是什么？

④ 你如何面对他人的批评？

⑤ 同事误解了你，你一般怎么做？

……

(8) 典型问题：你能为我们做些什么，而其他面试者无法做到？

面试官希望知道你与其他面试者的不同，即你的独一无二之处。事实上，这类问题是关于你是否真的了解自己或有自控能力的。认识自己或许是世界上最难的事情了，然而，你必须做到。唯有对自己有清晰的认识之后，你才知道自己的优势和独到之处。

参考回答：我的独到之处是有过硬的专业技能和建立良好客户关系的能力，这使得我可以为贵酒店争取到更多的回头客。

类似的问题如下所示。

① 你最大的优缺点分别是什么？

② 要是我告诉你我不喜欢你，你如何改变我的想法？

③ 如果你未通过这次面试，以后你会如何提升自己？

④ 虽然你工作努力，但是挣钱不如同事多，你会怎么办？

⑤ 你认为你适合什么样的工作，为什么？

⑥ 你为什么认为自己适合这份工作？

……

(9) 典型问题：你是个好队友吗？为什么？

面试官此处想了解你是否具备良好的团队合作精神。同时通过回答这类问题，你的交际技巧、人际关系、适应和组织能力也会得以考核。在酒店业，团队合作精神大多时候比个人能力更重要，因此从现在开始就应有意识地培养自己的团队精神。

参考回答：是的。我是系学生会成员之一，负责组织文体活动。为了组织好运动会和其他活动，我常常与同学合作，设计海报，安排场地等。他们都喜欢与我共事，因为我有很多好点子，而且乐于助人。

类似的问题如下所示。

① 当一位同事需要帮助的时候，描述一下他需要什么，在哪里，什么时候，你是如何帮助他的？举例说明。

② 你经常与陌生人说话吗？或只是常常与亲密的好友交流？

③ 你与同学相处如何？

④ 你更喜欢独立工作还是与他人合作？

⑤ 你认为你在同学中很受欢迎吗？为什么？

……

(10) 典型问题：你在学校所学与此工作有何联系？

此类问题旨在了解你的专业知识和技能。事先要准备好回答这类问题，例如，知道你在大学期间修过的且与该工作相关的课程的英文表达方式。

参考回答：我学过《现代酒店管理》、《酒店英语》、《客房管理》等相关课程。此外上学期间我在学院四星级酒店顶岗实习一个月，这一切使我受益良多，也为该工作做好了准备。

相关问题如下所示。

① 你如何确保各项标准在酒店中得以实施？

② 质量是旅游行业的首要标准。你如何保证高质量？

③ 大学期间你学过哪些跟酒店有关的科目或课程？

④ 你有哪些与酒店业相关的证书？

⑤ 关于××岗位，你具备哪些相应的技能？

⑥ 说出三件你从学校学到的而且可以应用到该工作中的事情。

⑦ 学校里的什么事情使你最兴奋？

……

在有些面试中面试官还可能问到这样的问题，“你有什么问题问我们吗？”不要急于询问报酬或奖励的情况。最好是问一下有关酒店提供的培训项目或进修机会的问题，这可以展示你的进取心，再就是你更关注工作机会本身，而不是只关心可以挣多少钱。

3.3 回答问题的原则

回答面试问题与课堂上或日常生活中回答问题截然不同。正如前文所述，面试官提问的每一个问题都带有动机和期待的回答。因此，知道如何回答每个问题非常重要而且有用。为了给出满意的回答，给面试官留下深刻的印象，你应该遵循几项回答问题的原则，下面将予以讨论。

(1) 典型问题：你期待什么样的报酬？

关于这个问题，首先你必须明白问题本身是什么意思，尤其是英文 remuneration 是什么意思？如果你没听懂问题或面试官说得太快，没跟上，千万不要根据自己听到的只言片语和个人理解回答问题。请面试官再说一遍或解释一下，直到你听懂问题为止。不要不好意思问。问的方法如图 3.2 所示。

a：“请重复一下您的问题好吗？我没听清。谢谢”

b：“请您再说一遍好吗？”

c：“请您解释一下问题好吗？”

当没听懂问题或没听清的时候……

图 3.2

其次，还要考虑面试官的动机：为什么他或她要问这个问题?面试官期待的并非一个数字，而是想了解你对报酬和工作的态度：哪个对你更重要？

参考回答：报酬很重要，不过我还年轻，对我来说，机会和工作本身对我的职业发展更为重要。

> 总之，回答问题的第一原则是听懂问题，明确面试官的提问动机。

(2) 典型问题：你为什么选择酒店管理作为你的专业？

回答：父母告诉我酒店业发展迅速，很有前途。毕业后找个好工作的机会多，所以我选了这个专业。或者，很多同学朋友选了这个专业，所以我也选了。

如果你的回答诸如此类，你留给面试官的印象就是缺乏独立性。这不太好。面试官希望雇佣那些可以独立思考和工作的人。

参考回答：酒店业发展迅速，给那些有志于投身该行业的人提供了大量机会。我相信，凭借对该行业的兴趣和个人努力，无论是在大学期间的酒店管理专业学习中还是未来的工作中我都可以表现得很好。

> 因此，回答问题时遵循的第二个原则是展示出你的独立性和个性。

(√) 我觉得/我认为/在我看来/个人观点/对我而言……

(×) 我妈妈/我姐姐/我哥哥告诉我做……

图 3.3

(3) 典型问题：你的朋友同学如何描述你？

回答：我所有的朋友同学都很喜欢我。他们喜欢跟我玩，一起分享事情。我很受他们欢迎。

这样的回答并不提倡，因为面试者没有正面回答问题。为了通过英文面试，你最好了解一下中西文化的特点。

西方文化可以比作比萨饼，观点呈现在面上，很直观清晰；中国文化更像饺子，细节包裹着观点(饺子馅——核心的内容包裹在里面)。

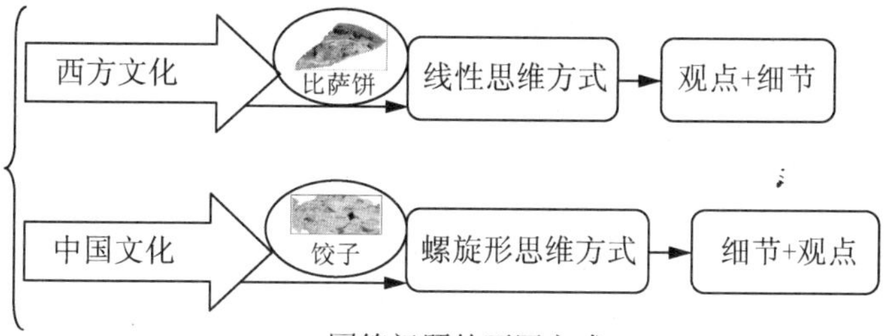

回答问题的不同方式

图 3.4

参考回答：他们说我是一个热心和有责任心的人。当他们遇到麻烦时，都愿意跟我说。

当参加英语面试时，记得用英语的思维方式思考和回答问题。需遵循的第三个原则是——首先陈述观点，然后决定是否进行进一步解释。

(4) 典型问题：如果你有 100 万美元可以捐献，你会捐给谁？

要是你的回答是“捐给穷人”，这样的回答就有些泛泛了。面试官更期待具体的回答或举例说明，这样可以获得更多的信息。如果你的回答过于宽泛，面试官可能会不知所云。

图 3.5

参考回答：要是我有这么一大笔钱，我会捐给教育机构，这样穷人家的孩子也可以受教育。或是捐给动物保护组织用于保护稀有动物。

因此面试时还应遵循这样的原则：回答问题尽量具体，不要过于宽泛。

(5) 典型问题：良好的服务对你来说指什么？

回答：良好的服务是指我要一直面带微笑，尽可能为顾客提供足够好的服务。

这或许是一个完整的回答，或许也不是，这取决于面试时的具体情况。给出观点后是否需要进行进一步的解释要看面试官的反应。陈述观点结束后，要注意面试官的反应，如果他/她等着你的解释，继续回答。一般来说，面试官都期待你解释一下“为什么”。

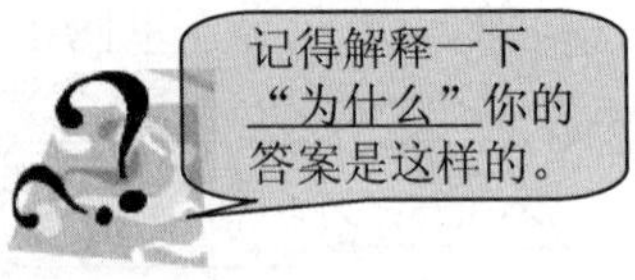

图 3.6

参考回答：对我来说，良好的服务是指我要一直面带微笑，为顾客尽可能提供足够好的服务。因为微笑是最美的语言，可以缩短人与人之间的距离。作为酒店员工，为顾客服务是我们的天职。我将始终微笑服务，让顾客满意。

总之，你的回答应该是回答+1，即记得解释一下为什么你的回答是这样的。

(6) 大学里你最不喜欢哪门课？

你最大的缺点是什么？

回答：我最不喜欢大学语文，因为我觉得很无聊，学语文都这么多年了，我觉得没有必要在大学再花费一年学语文。

我最大的缺点是我很懒。(或我很粗心或我上课常常迟到……)

遇到类似第一个这样的问题，不要抱怨某门课程所谓的太无聊或太难了。关于第二个问题，不要不经思考就说出你的缺点。上述回答显然是很不恰当的，因为他们传递出的信息很消极，面试官会觉得你将来一定也会抱怨工作或同事，他们不会因为你的懒惰、粗心或不守时而录用你。

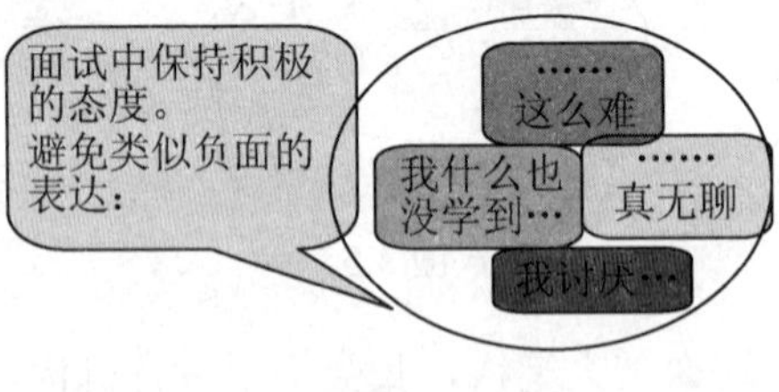

图 3.7

参考回答：刚上大学的时候，我对大学语文兴趣不大，不过慢慢地我意识到每一门课程都有其存在的理由，而且很重要。从那时起，我开始阅读中文小说，参加诗社。

我觉得我最大的缺点是太过于细心。按要求完成工作后我总是会再认真地检查一遍。有时这使我很困扰，我觉得自己都给自己带来压力了。

切记面试时保持积极的态度，这将大大有助于你最后获得工作机会。

(7) 典型问题：你在职业发展方面毕生的梦想是什么？

回答：我一直希望可以成为五星级酒店的经理，因为酒店管理是我的专业，我喜欢在酒店工作，我想把自己所有的才干投入酒店业，最终取得一点成就……

上述回答缺少一个好的结尾。面试者可以继续回答，而且可以说很多。这里要讨论的是如何恰当地结束回答。有两个方式可以参考，一是重复一下问题或自己的观点：这就是我对……的观点或理解；另一种方式是通过眼神交流或点头、微笑等面部表情示意面试官，然后结束回答。当然，最后的选择是被面试官打断。

参考回答：我一直希望可以成为五星级酒店的经理，因为酒店管理是我的专业，我喜欢在酒店工作，这就是我毕生的梦想。

如何结束你的回答……

1. 重复一下观点。
2. 用眼神或其他面部表情告诉面试官。

图 3.8

当你想结束回答时，重复一下你的观点或用微笑、眼神交流等给面试官一个提示。

此外，在面试结束时，记得微笑着表示你的感谢，然后起身离开。

第 4 章　不同面试问题分析

本教程中涉及的品牌酒店多数位于海外或中国的大城市，例如北京、上海等，因此为了方便面试和提高面试效率这些酒店会采取多种不同的面试方式，包括电话面试、视频面试、群面和单面等。本节将分析如何针对不同面试中的问题进行准备，为参加面试的您提供更多的面试技巧。

3.4.1　面试程序

品牌酒店宣布招聘计划后，会收到许多求职信，对于人力资源部工作人员来说，面试所有的应聘者是不易的，因此面试前他们会先筛选简历，选出部分求职者参加面试。以下是两份英文简历模板，供您制作简洁准确的简历，以其给面试官留下深刻印象：

一般来说，筛选完简历之后，品牌酒店会通过电话或网络(具体来说，是通过联网的带有摄像头和耳麦的电脑进行)进行面试，这就是电话面试或视频面试。一方面，这种面试可以节省酒店面试成本，另一方面，通过电话或网络，酒店可以更多地了解应聘者，包括简历的真实性、个人背景、表达和交流能力等，这可以帮助酒店选出最适合参加下一轮面对面面试的人员。

简 历

个人信息

姓:	名:
出生日期:	籍贯:
性别:	婚姻状况:
电话号码:	电子邮箱:

主修课程

教育背景

所获奖励

工作经历

英语技能

计算机技能

图 3.9

简 历

个人信息

姓:
名:
出生日期:
专业:
电话号码:
邮箱地址:

照片

教育背景

工作经历

奖学金及其它奖励

个人优势

其他

图 3.10

面对面面试最常采用的方式是群面和单面。群面指一组应聘者同时参加面试，可能会要求回答相同的问题。品牌酒店群面中通常提问大众化问题，面试官经比较后选出更合适的应聘者，事实证明群面是招聘的有效方式。单面指每次只有一位面试者参加的面试，面试官最后做出用人选择时常常采用这种面试方式，他们提问的问题更加具体，与酒店行业、个人职业发展、工作经历、申请的职位等相关。

3.4.2 不同面试问题分析

根据上述部分，不同的面试因功能不同，提问的问题也不同。根据多年来对品牌酒店(尤其是第一章提到的酒店)面试的记录得知，不同面试中涉及的问题大体分为三类：电话或视频面试中的问题主要基于简历；群面的问题比较大众化；单面的问题都是与工作和酒店行业紧密相关的专业性问题。

1. 电话或视频面试

电话或视频面试中，面试官提问的问题往往与简历相关，例如：

(1) 简历中提到你的专业是酒店管理，请告诉我关于这个专业你学到了什么？

(2) 你如何获得一等奖学金的？

(3) 你认为学好英语的好方法是什么？

(4) 你有做兼职，请告诉我你的岗位职责是什么？

(5) 大学里你取得的最大的成绩是什么？

……

此外，应聘者接电话或挂断电话时应该非常礼貌，以下是一些建议：接电话时可以这样打招呼："你好，先生/女士/***先生/***女士/, 我是***"；结束时可以使用这样的表达："谢谢您打给我""谢谢您给我这次机会""你拿出时间面试我，考虑我，非常感谢""和您通话很高兴"。如果确实不方便接听电话，可以做出解释，例如"谢谢您打给我电话，不过现在周围很嘈杂，我听不清楚，请留下电话号码一会儿我打给您好吗？"

2. 群面

面试官在群面中会问一些一般性的问题，群面更像谈话，例如：

(1) 请用英语介绍一下自己好吗？

① 你的英文名字是什么？ 你为什么选择这个名字？

② 你多大了？

③ 请问照片上这个人是谁？你和他是什么关系？

(面试者按要求准备一些照片，面试官会就此提问)

(2) 你问什么想去国外工作？

(3) 你为什么想来我们酒店工作？

(4) 你的优缺点各是什么？

(5) 你能用三个词描述自己吗？

(6) 你的朋友/同事如何评价你？

(7) 你有哪些爱好？/ 课余时间你都做些什么？

(8) 你的英语老师是谁？请描述一下他/她。

(9) 你取得的最大成绩是什么？

……

在该部分中，表达能力和交际能力是考量的最重要的两方面，因此应聘者应多花时间，努力提高个人交际能力。

3. 单面

从有关酒店业、酒店管理、酒店岗位的问题到有关应聘者的工作经历、专业知识、职业发展等的问题都会在单面中出现，典型问题如下：

(1) 你想申请的职位是什么？

(2) 你为什么想当服务生/客房服务员/收银员/帮厨？

① 作为服务生/客房服务员/收银员/帮厨工作很辛苦，你如何做好这份工作？

② 你实习时工作是门童，现在为什么申请客房服务员一职呢？

(3) 你认为什么是最好的管理？

(4) 你认为这份工作重要的部分是什么？

……

面试官旨在测试应聘者的专业资格，专业知识和个人潜力。因此应聘者在参加面试前应长期做准备，他们可以通过上课、自学、在酒店兼职、做好职业规划等方式。

结语

进行充分的准备才能在遇到机会时赢得最后的工作机会。充分的准备指要认识自己，了解要申请的工作，坚信自己确实需要这份工作，而且工作也的确适合自己。机会指面试本身。本章介绍了面试问题的种类、面试官的提问动机和面试者回答问题时遵循的原则，所有这些都归结为面试技巧。相信有了这些技巧，就可以顺利通过面试，赢得工作。

本章思考题

下面是一场小组模拟面试的实录。面试官是一位来自阿联酋迪拜五星级酒店的人力资源经理，该酒店计划在中国招聘 20 名餐饮部服务生和 10 名客房服务员。他正在面试 3 名候选人，一个是安吉拉，旅游英语专业大二的学生，其他两人是玛丽和珍妮，她们都是酒店管理专业的学生。首先通读该实录，然后分析面试者的回答，看一看他们的回答是否恰当。然后和同学一起，以小组为单位，进行模拟面试练习。

首先，3 名面试同学敲了敲门，听到“请进”后走入面试房间。

面试者：早上好，先生。

面试官：早上好，请坐。请说一下你们的中英文名字。

安吉拉：我叫李丽，安吉拉是我的英文名。

玛丽：我叫王华，英文名为玛丽。

珍妮：我是刘梅，英文名为珍妮。

面试官：谢谢。你好，安吉拉，你申请哪个岗位？

安吉拉：我申请的是服务生。

面试官：你为什么想来我们酒店工作？

安吉拉：因为我觉得迪拜的酒店业发展迅速，在贵酒店工作可以给我最好的机会运用我所学到的知识。

面试官：你有工作经验吗？

安吉拉：是的。去年暑假，我在一家大的餐厅干了近两个月的服务生。这段经历培养了我的责任心，锻炼了我做事灵活和敏锐的性格。

面试官：珍妮，你好，你如何理解“服务意识”？

珍妮：不好意思，我不明白你在说什么，请再说一遍好吗？

面试官：“服务意识”。

珍妮：……?

面试官：“服务意识”，依据你的工作经历和所学知识，你如何理解“服务意识”？

珍妮：我认为保持微笑很重要，这可以使顾客感到温暖。

面试官：玛丽，你好，你申请了哪个岗位？

玛丽：我想当一名服务生。

面试官：在 F & B?

玛丽：……？

面试官：你想在哪个部门工作？

玛丽：我想当一名服务生。

面试官：你知道服务生属于哪个部门吗？

玛丽：我想在餐饮部工作。

面试官：对了，F & B 是餐饮部的简称。玛丽，你为什么想出国工作？

玛丽：我认为迪拜的酒店业很发达，出国可以提高我的英语水平，出国是件很荣幸的事情，我想在贵酒店提升自己。

面试官：珍妮，能告诉我你想去阿联酋酒店工作的目的吗？

珍妮：是的。去年，我参加了全运会的服务工作。我在一家四星级酒店做客房服务员，关于如何成为合格的客房服务员，我学到了很多。

面试官：但是还记得我的问题吗？你听懂问题了吗？

珍妮：关于工作经验……

面试官：安吉拉，请重复一下我刚才的问题。

安吉拉：关于去阿联酋工作？

面试官：你为什么想去阿联酋工作？

安吉拉：去阿联酋可以提高我的技能，锻炼自己。

面试官：在哪些方面？

安吉拉：在工作过程中锻炼自己。

面试官：好的……玛丽，回答同样的问题。

玛丽：我认为年轻的时候应该尽全力为未来做好准备，例如出国锻炼自己，就是这样。

面试官：安吉拉，我知道你的专业不是酒店管理。

安吉拉：是的。

面试官：但是其他两位是，她们已经学过很多关于酒店管理的课程，跟你比，她们很有优势。你如何说服我录用你而不是她们俩呢？

安吉拉：谢谢您的提问。虽然我的专业不是酒店管理，但是我有工作经验，并且知道服务生的工作流程，知道如何为客人服务。我的专业是旅游英语，我认为如果出国工作语言是我的一项优势。同时我学东西很快。刚去餐厅做兼职的第一天，经理教给我如何排放餐具，如何为客人服务，我照做了，经理很满意，说，“做得好，你学得很快”。

面试官：好的。你好，玛丽，与其他两位相比，你的优势是什么？

玛丽：抱歉。

面试官：你的意思是……告诉我，与她们两位相比，你的特别突出之处是什么？

玛丽：我认为我工作努力，大家有目共睹，这是我的一个优势。

面试官：你呢，珍妮？

珍妮：我不是很聪明，但我很努力。因为我坚信有付出就有回报。一个人的潜力远远超过他已经实现的一切。此外，我喜欢交朋友，我认为朋友是生活中重要的一部分。

面试官：好的，安吉拉，在你的工作中，曾经遇到难缠的顾客吗？

安吉拉：是的，有一天，一位客人把我叫过去，大声说，“这鱼怎么回事，一点都不新鲜？”我觉得很尴尬，菜不是我炒的，我什么也不知道。

面试官：那你做出了什么回应？

安吉拉：我说我非常抱歉，然后给他换了另外一盘。

面试官：顾客满意了吗？

安吉拉：是的，他对我的工作很满意。

面试官：当你的老板做错了事，而且确实做错了，你也知道，那你会怎么办？

安吉拉：不好意思，请再说一遍好吗？

面试官：你的老板犯了个错误，你知道，他绝对做错了，你会怎么做？

安吉拉：我不会直接告诉他。我将用自己的方式证明他错了。

面试官：玛丽，你呢，你会怎么做？

玛丽：我将用实际行动告诉他错了。

面试官：好的，就到这里了，谢谢。

面试者：谢谢。

面试官：再见。

面试者：再见。

第4章 面试注意事项

4.1 常见错误

1. 语音

如第 1 章所述，语音也是影响口头交流的音素之一。蹩脚的语音会使交流中断，交流困难或引起误解，而流畅、自然、地道的发音能使面试者获得自信。

为了改进应试者的语音，我们需要分析语音错误。

(1) 元音混淆

(2) 词尾音过重

由于汉语普通话中没有清音，中国的英语学习者往往过分强调词尾音，但在英语中却有 9 个清音，比如[p] [t] [k] [f] [s] [θ]。相当多的中国学习者将这些音当成浊音对待，例如，他们会说“I help<u>er</u> him to read the book<u>er</u>.”。

此外，中国人还将词尾的浊辅音和元音说得过重，拖延这些音，这使得这些音过于响亮，甚至于比重读音节的音还要响亮。由于这些变化都发生在词尾，口语的连续就突然中断了，而这些过重的音妨碍了一个单词顺畅而自然地向随后的单词过渡，其结果是，口语中的韵律和流畅消失了，这样便出现了“中国式的英语 ”。

(3) 除了词尾音过重外，中国的学生还过分加重非重读音节的音，尤其是弱化音。比如，过去的结尾-ed 跟在/t/或/d/后面总是一个弱化的音节，然后中国人往往说的过重，这样的单词如“visited”“waited” 和 “handed”.

(4) 而且，值得注意的是，英语为母语的人士往往是在有意义的意群之间停顿，讲话听起来显得自然而流畅，然而，英语学习者往往是在单词间停顿，从而引起听者的困惑，使得理解变得麻烦，困难。比如在句子*“As a result I really learnt a lot about how to be a qualified room attendant”中*。英语人士是这样说：

“ As a re’sult / I really ‘learnt a ‘lot/ about ‘how to be a ‘qualified room attendant.” 而英语学习者却使这样说：

“ As a result ‘I / ‘really/ ‘learnt / a ‘lot /’about/ ‘how/ ‘to be a qualified room/ ‘attendant”.

然而，有些学习者总认为，他们说得越快，别人就以为他们说得越流利。必须指出，没有适当连读、停顿、重音或弱化音的匆忙表述，其结果是误解，甚至不能交流。并且，由于语言不够好，赶不上这样的语速而暴露了自己。

4.2 不妥举止

面试官对应试者将作全面评价，所以，应试者的方方面面诸如面部表情、目光接触、形象、肢体语言等都是面试官的关注所在。应试者应该注意些什么呢？下面说明应试者应该做和不该做的事情。

1. 应该做的事情

(1) 了解所申请工作的酒店和酒店集团。在面试准备中，应试者可以搜查有关该酒店和酒店集团的信息。网络上有大量的信息可利用。尽量收集有关该酒店或酒店集团文化的信息，也可向熟悉的人了解面试的有关情况。

(2) 着职业装，适当打扮。着装打扮反映了你的职业素养。应试者的形象面试官在和你说话握手前就注意到了。为了留下良好的第一印象，应试者需要着职业装，一定要把社交形象(比较随意，且一般都是如此)和职业展示区分开来。

你的体味(即使闻起来不错)也是应注意的。应试者喜欢用的香水或古龙水可能会起反作用，从而使应试者失去就业的机会。

(3) 提前 10 分钟到达面试现场。关注自己准备的材料，而且这 10 分钟也能使应试者做好心理准备。

(4) 对面试官彬彬有礼，尊重，友好。即使你不喜欢面试官的言行，然而，这时他的地位比自己高。对他表示尊敬也意味着即使你在工作中有不同意见也愿意遵从上司。

(5) 与面试官目光接触。目光接触是一种非语言交流。正如中国的成语所说，“眼睛是心灵的窗户。”通过目光接触，面试官会观察到应试者的内心想法和情感。因此，怎样强调其重要性也不为过。应试者应重视非语言的表达，表现出兴趣和自信。

(6) 保持从容坐姿，不要显得局促不安。不论是走、站还是坐都要保持职业化的姿势，直到你从面试官的视野里消失为止。

(7) 回答每一个问题，可能时提供例证。对于面试官的提问仅回答“是”或“不是”是远不能令人满意的。当被提问时，应试者应首先给出一个明确的回答，然后再做必要的简明、具体的解释。

(8) 如果没有听明白，就礼貌地请面试官重复或解释问题。有时候听不明白是众所周知的。这种现象也常反生在英语是母语的人之间。所以，如果在交流中错过了要点，不要欺骗自己，应有礼貌地询问面试官。

(9) 回答提问时，用完整的句子。当应试者使用了过多的不完整句子时，面试官很容易看出应试者的英语水平有限，尽管不完整的句子也常在会话中使用。

(10) 秉持诚实的态度，因为面试官随时会发现谎言。“诚实为上策”。即使得到这份工作，也难以掩盖谎言。欺骗行为会伤害自己，使自己在酒店的信誉扫地。

(11) 保持自己的特性。在面试中突出自己的特性尤其是优点。不要按照别人期待的样子去做。即使得到了这份工作，人们也会发现你到底是一个什么样的人。

(12) 对提供的工作岗位表现出热情和兴趣来。对面试机会表现出兴奋和高涨的热情，并展示自己的工作能力，这将给面试官留下良好的印象。

(13) 从正面展示自己。应试者应该向面试官展示自己是位可以合作的人选。尽管人无完人，但是没有必要主动说出自己的不足。应该利用这次机会在有限的时间内尽量展示自己的优点和长处。

(14) 准备几个问题，询问事先没有查询到的有关该酒店或酒店集团的情况。面试的大部分时间是面试官向应试者提问，然而，交流是双向的，互相的。偶尔询问面试官不仅能表现出应试者的兴趣，也能引起面试官对应试者的兴趣。

(15) 面试结束要有礼貌地离开。离开前友好地表示谢意和辞别。面朝面试官轻掩房门，并会心地向其微笑。

2. 避免做的事情

(1) 事先不要吃大蒜，不要咀嚼食物，不要吸烟。令人不快的气味会让你周围的人以及面试官感到沮丧。这种场合嚼口香糖也会令人不高兴。

(2) 不要开启手机。最好不要把手机带入面试现场，不期而至的信息或电话会分散你面试的注意力。而对面试官说“对不起”为时已晚，更不要说把手机遗忘在现场，它会表明你是个粗心大意的人。

(3) 走、站、坐的姿势要端正，不要显得无精打采，坐着时不要靠椅背，不要僵硬地坐在椅子边沿。你无精打采、靠椅背、或僵硬的姿势表明你对这份工作缺乏热情，紧张或懒散。作为一个酒店服务业的从业人员，这些举动会给你带来负面的影响。

(4) 不要抱怨别人或先前的工作。抱怨与你相处的人或你以前做的工作会给面试官留下一个这样的印象：你不是那种他期待的与人合作的人。

(5) 不要说“我很紧张。”事实上，适当的紧张有助于你对任务的关注。处在你这样的情景中，人人都会或多或少地紧张。但是过分紧张会对你的表现带来负面的影响。即便你说你紧张，面试官也不会原谅你。相反，他会以为你不够自信。

(6) 不要撒谎。事实上，适当的紧张有助于你对任务的关注。处在你这样的情景中，人人都会或多或少地紧张。但是过分紧张会对你的表现带来负面的影响。即便你说你紧张，面试官也不会原谅你。相反，他会以为你不够自信。

(7) 不要说自己只想到酒店提高英语水平然后辞职回国。事实上，适当的紧张有助于你对任务的关注。处在你这样的情景中，人人都会或多或少地紧张。但是过分紧张会对你的表现带来负面的影响。即便你说你紧张，面试官也不会原谅你。相反，他会以为你不够自信。

(8) 不要表现出对薪水特别在意。面试官未提起薪水，不要询问薪水的事。薪水无疑是重要的，但是不应该作为你首要考虑的问题，尤其对于一个年轻人来说，应该把提高职业技能作为首要的问题来考虑。

(9) 不要说申请的岗位“太难了”。这似乎显得你对应对棘手的局面或克服工作中的阻碍没有信心。用’具有挑战性’这个词更有积极的意义。最好是让面试官相信，你随时准备应对挑战。

(10) 不要在话还没有说完就起身离开。在没有辞别前不要迈步离开。如果没有把最后的话都说完就离开，这看来你想要尽快逃离现场，表明你不够成熟。

附录 B

世界著名酒店集团简介

我们的培训主要是针对国外酒店面试的，下面将对以下 5 个世界著名酒店集团的发展史、企业文化及旗下品牌做一个简介。

(1) 卓美亚酒店与度假酒店；

(2) 洲际国际酒店集团；

(3) 雅高集团；

(4) 希尔顿酒店集团；

(5) 喜达屋国际酒店集团。

1. 卓美亚酒店与度假酒店

(1) 发展史。卓美亚酒店与度假酒店隶属于卓美亚集团，堪称世界上最奢华、最具创新意识的酒店，已荣获无数国际旅游奖项。集团始建于 1997 年，立志通过打造世界一流的奢华酒店及度假酒店，成为行业领袖。

卓美亚 Beach Hotel 的落成，赋予了豪华酒店全新的定义。随后，世界最奢华的卓美亚 Burj Al Arab 开业。如今的帆船酒店依然光彩夺目，始终代表着最顶级的奢华体验。2000 年，卓美亚 Emirates Towers 获得商务旅行者的普遍赞誉。伦敦贝尔格莱维亚的卓美亚 Carlton Tower 和卓美亚 Lowndes Hotel 相继以全新面貌亮相。2004 年，卓美亚 Madinat 在迪拜海滨巍然耸起，三大精品酒店形成别具一格的阿拉伯风情之地。不久，卓美亚 Bab Al Shams Desert Resort and Spa 在沙漠腹地崛起，宛若沙丘之中的世外桃源。2006 年，集团又投入另一项宏伟工程，将纽约卓美亚 Essex House 翻修一新，打造成为美国最奢华绚丽的酒店。

卓美亚集团的主营业务是管理豪华酒店及度假酒店，同时还管理着卓美亚 Living，豪华的高级服务式公寓；知名水疗品牌泰丽丝水疗中心(Talise)；餐饮部门卓美亚 Restaurants；精彩连连的疯狂维迪水上乐园(Wild Wadi Waterpark)；卓美亚阿联酋酒店管理学院；以及拥有 15 家零售店及购物门户网站的卓美亚 Retail。

(2) 旗下品牌及地域分布。

迪拜：卓美亚 Burj Al Arab，卓美亚 Beach Hotel，卓美亚 Emirates Towers，卓美亚 Madinat，卓美亚 Bab Al Shams Desert Resort & Spa，卓美亚 The Meydan，卓美亚 Zabeel Saray

伦敦：卓美亚 Carlton，卓美亚 Lowndes Hotel

纽约：卓美亚 Essex House

(3) 经营理念。

核心理念：尽享非凡

品牌核心：

① 始终在第一时间微笑着问候客人；

② 永不直接、生硬地拒绝客人的请求；

③ 尊重同事，以诚待人。

卓美亚指导方针与愿望：

诚实守信：我们做每一件事都秉着诚实守信的原则。我们言行一致，言出必行，树立团队的信心。

团队合作：我们本着互利互惠的态度，提倡开放式沟通和相互支持，为共同的目标而努力。我们尊重文化差异，自主自强。

认可：我们确保个人的需求和成功得到支持和认可。

创新：我们开阔思路，虚心向前，挑战传统思维，改进工作流程，以比竞争对手更快的速度将创新理念付诸实践。

持续发展：我们为员工的成长和业务的繁荣发展提供良好的环境。

以人为本：我们悉心关怀员工、客户和商业伙伴，而他们也将我们视为首选合作伙伴。

我们的愿望：打造世界级的豪华国际酒店及酒店管理公司，通过对股东、员工、客户、商业合作伙伴与所有者的殷切付出，致力于成为所涉猎领域的行业领导者。

2. 洲际国际酒店集团

(1) 发展史。洲际集团成立于 1777 年，是一个全球化的酒店集团，它是世界上客房拥有量最大的酒店集团，在全球 100 多个国家和地区经营着超过 4500 家酒店，超过 650000 间客房。

1777 年 Bass 在英国创立了一个酿酒厂，后来发展成为英国顶级酿造者之一。

1876 年 Bass 的商标红三角成为英国第一个注册商标。

20 世纪 60 年代 Bass 收购了一些知名的酿酒公司，成为英国最大的酿酒商，也拥有最多的酒馆。

1988 年 Bass 购入 Holiday Inns International，开始涉足宾馆业。

1989 年由于禁酒 Bass 开始减少酒吧数量，其余的资金用于宾馆发展。

1990 年购入 North American Holiday Inn 和 Holiday Inn，酒店开始进入国际化。

1991 年推出假日快捷(Holiday Inn Express)，弥补服务细分中的不足。

1994 年推出皇冠假日(Crowne Plaza)，迎合高层次消费者。同年拥有的小酒吧转化成小旅馆，迎合英国日益增长的外出就餐市场。

1997 年推出 Staybridge Suites，迎合高消费长住市场，发展迅速，在美国已有 50 多家。

1998 年购入 InterContinental hotel company，增加了另一个高消费品牌。

2000 年在澳大利亚买入 Southern Pacific Hotels Corporation (SPHC)，确立了在亚太地区酒店业的领头地位。同年将 Bass 酿酒厂以 23 亿英镑的价格卖给比利时一家酒厂，然后更名为 Six Continents PLC。

2001 年以 6.25 亿英镑的价格卖出 988 家小的不知名的酒吧，以 8.1 亿英镑的价格买入 European Posthouse chain of hotels，其战略位置十分重要，在将其转换为 Holiday Inn 后，巩固了 Holiday Inn 在英国和欧洲大陆的地位。同年以 2.41 亿英镑购入 InterContinental Hong Kong，巩固了其在中国和亚太高消费市场的地位。

2002 年集团的酒店业和软饮料业与零售业(Mitchells & Butlers plc)分离。

2003 年增加了一个中级长住酒店品牌 Candlewood。

2004 年推出 Indigo，提供实惠精品屋住宿。

2005 年借鉴 Staybridge Suites 在美国的成功实例，在英国推出 Staybridge Suites。同年清理集团对软饮料(Britvic plc.)的控股，成为专注于旅馆的公司。

2006 年在日本与 All Nippon Airways (ANA)合资，使其成为日本最大的国际酒店经营者。

2007 年大力发展 Holiday Inn 品牌，计划 2008 年在美国开始，2010 年底结束。

(2) 经营理念-制胜之道：①做正确的事情；②关怀顾客；③目标高远；④求同存异；⑤团队合作，协作共赢。

(3) 旗下品牌(7 个)。洲际酒店(InterContinental Hotels & Resorts)、皇冠假日(Crowne Plaza)、Hotel Indigo、假日酒店(Holiday Inn)、假日快捷(Holiday Inn Express)、Staybridge Suites and Candlewood Suites。

INTERCONTINENTAL.
HOTELS & RESORTS

洲际酒店及度假村是旗下最知名的酒店品牌，遍布全球 60 多个国家的主要城市，为商务和休闲旅游者提供最高等级的服务和设施。

CROWNE PLAZA
HOTELS & RESORTS

皇冠假日酒店及度假村是一个充满活力的国际酒店品牌，遍布世界近 60 个国家，它为追求简约优雅的高品位的商务和休闲旅游者设计，并为其提供上等的住宿条件。

Hotel Indigo 是一个崭新的创新型的品牌，专为寻求个性化设施的时尚旅游者设计。酒店遍布整个美国的城区、中等城镇和郊区，靠近商业中心、餐馆和娱乐场所。

假日酒店为商务和休闲旅游者提供依靠、友好的服务，现代化的设施和超值体验。不管是在全球的小城镇还是大城市，僻静的公路沿线还是喧嚣的机场附近，你都能找到假日酒店。

快捷假日酒店干净、简单，令人耳目一新，为客人提供舒适、便利和物有所值的体验。它是这个市场领域中发展最快的酒店品牌之一。

Staybridge 套房式酒店是一个全套房式的酒店品牌，面向寻求家庭式设施的商务常驻者及休闲旅游者。

Candlewood 套房式酒店提供高质量的住宿条件，满足了中档市场连续多晚住店的商务及休闲旅游者的需要。

3. 雅高集团

(1) 发展史。雅高集团是全球最大的酒店管理集团之一及欧洲酒店业的领导者，全线覆盖从奢华型到经济型酒店的市场。它在全球 90 多个国家拥有 4000 多家酒店，经营 500000 多间客房。

(2) 企业文化——核心价值观：①创新是我们的商标；②进取精神是我们成长的动力；③绩效是我们持续成功的关键；④尊重是我们维持关系的基础；⑤信任是我们管理的根基。

(3) 旗下品牌。雅高集团经营着 14 种从奢华型到经济型不同特色的品牌，他们的服务质量得到世界的认可，品牌包括索菲特 Sofitel、铂尔曼 Pullman、美爵 MGallery、诺富特 Novotel、Suite Novotel、美居 Mercure、ibis、all seasons、Etap hotel、hotelF1、Motel6，还有 Thalassa sea & spa 和 Lenôtre。雅高的不同品牌可以满足各个商务及休闲客人的不同需求。

4. 希尔顿全球

(1) 发展史。希尔顿全球为商务及休闲旅游者提供最一流的住宿、服务、设施和价值。自 1919 年康莱德 • 希尔顿在得克萨斯州买下他的第一家酒店后，酒店业便在不同地域发展起来，他创造了新颖的酒店和旅行理念并运用创新性的科技提高客人的体验。现在希尔顿酒店集团已经成为全球领先的酒店集团，经营着不同类型的酒店，从奢华的全方位服务酒店和度假酒店到长住套房以及中等价位酒店。

(2) 企业文化。

远景：让地球充满酒店业带来的光与温暖。

使命：我们要成为超群绝伦的全球性酒店集团，成为客人、团队成员和业主的首选。

价值观：

H Hospitality 酒店业——我们对为客人提供卓越的体验充满激情。

I Integrity 诚实守信——我们每时每刻都做正确的事。

L Leadership 领导——我们是我们行业和社区的领导者。

T Teamwork 团队——做任何事情都体现我们的团队精神。

O Ownership 所有权——我们是我们行动和决策的主人。

N NOW 现在——我们带着一种紧迫感和纪律感来经营。

(3) 旗下品牌。希尔顿全球为客人提供 10 个优越的酒店品牌，在 81 个国家拥有

3600 多家酒店，包括奢华的全方位服务酒店和度假酒店、舒适的长住套房，优质的中等价位酒店和令人放松的分时度假酒店。旗下品牌主要包括希尔顿酒店及度假酒店、康拉德酒店及度假酒店、Waldorf Astoria 酒店及度假酒店、希尔顿逸林、大使套房酒店(Embassy Suites Hotels)、希尔顿花园客栈(Hilton Garden Inn)、汉普顿旅馆(Hampton Inn & Suites)、家木套房(Homewood Suites by Hilton)，Home2 套房和希尔顿度假俱乐部(Hilton Grand Vacations)。所有的品牌都参与世界级长住客项目——希尔顿奖励计划(Hilton HHonors)。

忠诚度项目

奢华型品牌

全方位服务品牌

特定服务品牌

分时度假品牌

5. 喜达屋酒店集团

(1) 发展史。

1991 年由一些持有众多资产净值、专门从事不动产购置的家庭出资，喜达屋资本集团合作伙伴在芝加哥成立。

1993 年喜达屋资本集团收购了其首批酒店，到 1994 年，它已在 30 多家酒店拥有自己的股份。

1995 年，一家在纽约证券交易所(NYSE)上市的酒店投资信托公司负债累累，它是不动产投资信托基金(REIT)的“双股”，喜达屋资本集团收购了此公司的控股权，将其更名为喜达屋膳宿公司(Starwood Lodging)。喜达屋股票当年飙升了 72.46%！

1997 年 9 月，喜达屋膳宿公司宣布了一项协议，拟用 18 亿美元收购威斯汀酒店及度假酒店。10 月，该公司宣布了另一协议，针对希尔顿的恶意收购，喜达屋膳宿公司作为白骑士拟用 143 亿美元收购 ITT 喜来登公司。喜达屋羽翼渐丰，逐步成为一家跨国公司。同年年底，喜达屋股票的升幅达 57.4%。

1998 年 1 月，喜达屋膳宿公司完成了对威斯汀酒店及度假酒店的收购。随着收购工作的结束，喜达屋膳宿公司也更名为喜达屋酒店及度假酒店。2 月，喜达屋结束了对 ITT 喜来登公司的收购。喜达屋的资产现包括遍布全球 70 多个国家和地区的 650 多家酒店及度假酒店。

喜达屋的首家酒店于 12 月在纽约开业。W 品牌的推出旨在展现一家独立、独特酒店的个性与特点，同时也是一种承诺，保证为商务旅行人员提供可信、高档的设施与服务。W 以随意优雅的客房和都市风格为特色。

1999 年喜达屋收购了一家分时度假公司——维斯塔那，藉此在方兴未艾的分时度假市场上崭露头角。之后，该公司更名为喜达屋分时度假公司，成为喜达屋集团赢利最多的公司之一。

喜达屋推出了喜达屋优先顾客(SPG®)计划，以丰厚的回报向酒店常宿旅客表示谢意。该计划大力推广其无日期限制、无入住人数限制的政策——这两项政策在业界均属首例！

威斯汀酒店引入了天梦之床(Heavenly Bed®)，该睡床以柔软的双垫层床垫、羽绒被褥和豪华、全白床单为特色。这一措施一举成功。

瑞吉品牌从纽约的一家酒店发展为 6 家，全部荣登 1999 年度 *Condé Nast Traveler* 金牌榜！

福朋喜来登集团酒店开设了其第 100 家酒店——加利福尼亚圣莫尼卡福朋喜来登集团酒店。

2001 年在第八届“世界旅游奖”颁奖典礼上，喜达屋酒店及度假酒店集团被授予“世界一流酒店集团”。

在第 13 届“Freddie 奖”投票评选中，SPG 计划连续第二次获得年度第一，该奖项为旅游业最权威的奖项。

威斯汀酒店将天梦之床(Heavenly Bath®)引入北美地区酒店，使得旅客在清晨醒来时都对该睡床无比留恋。喜达屋将威斯汀的天梦摇篮(Westin Heavenly Crib®)和福朋喜来登的甜梦摇篮引入了北美地区酒店。

2003 年喜达屋宣布，其美国和加拿大境内的喜来登、威斯汀和 W 酒店欢迎宠物狗入住。作为喜达屋 LTD (Love That Dog)计划中的一部分，4 条腿的客人将享受到豪华狗床和包括长绒浴袍、小狗玩具、犬齿信息等在内的各种服务。

喜来登酒店及度假酒店引入了喜来登甜梦之床(Sheraton Sweet Sleeper™ Bed)，该床配有 30cm 厚的高织 Sealy Posturepedic 长绒床垫、触感柔和的羽绒枕头和亚麻棉布床单。在促使该品牌一跃成为高档酒店的一些计划当中，这是最新的一项举措。

2005 年在第 17 届“Freddie 奖”投票评选活动中，SPG 计划连续第 6 年被评为美国和世界年度最佳计划。作为业界最受尊重的计划，SPG 计划不断取得成功。

2006 年喜达屋将艾美品牌及其旗下全部的管理酒店及特许权经营酒店收归旗下，主要位于欧洲及中东的 137 家酒店成为喜达屋集团的一部分。

2007 年喜达屋宣布其选择服务酒店类别中期待已久的新品牌：雅乐轩。经由创建 W 酒店的团队构思，雅乐轩将提高精选服务类别的标准，提供带有都市气息的阁楼式客房、经过改进的技术服务、适用于昼夜社交活动的室外观景区和活力四射的休息室外景观。

2008 年第一家雅乐轩在美国马萨诸塞州列克星敦开业。

2009 年喜达屋投资 60 亿美金用于增进喜来登复兴工程，全球 60 家新建和 120 家翻新的喜来登酒店及度假村从中受益，有 300 多家门廊、70000 间客房、100000 张床装葺一新，大堂休息区配备了品牌的独特网络。

2010 年，喜达屋为第 1000 家酒店的开业这个重要里程碑庆祝！千岛湖喜来登度假村在中国著名的千岛湖畔开业。

(2) 企业文化。

① 使命与价值观：在喜达屋，我们的使命宣言和价值观描述了我们做事的方式。我们致力于诚挚的合作，促进相互信任与尊重，并通过创新和革新来为公司树立崭新的形象，使这里成为最具乐趣的工作场所。

② 服务文化：我们相信，不仅仅在于我们做事的内容，而且还在于我们做事的方式。对客人满意度的承诺是喜达屋区别于其他集团的关键，它体现了好公司与顶级公司之间的差异。

③ 多元化与包容性：我们深信多元化和包容性不仅仅是说说，而是企业必须做到的。我们的成功需要不同类型的人才、观点和背景，我们一直竭力在这方面进行改善。

④ 融入社区(社区合作伙伴关系)：我们承认我们是全球社区的一部分，我们很重

视与社区的合作伙伴关系。我们知道优秀的企业对我们周围的世界能产生积极的影响。

⑤ 企业价值观。通过采取建立持久关系和忠诚度的行动更进一步；全球及公司所有团队的工作都要有团队协作的精神；通过进行正确的判断，尊重我们的社区、同事、业主、合作伙伴和环境，来做正确的事情。

(3) 旗下品牌，包括艾美(Le Méridien®)、Element℠ 酒店、雅乐轩酒店(Aloft℠ Hotels)、喜来登酒店及度假酒店(Sheraton® Hotels & Resorts)、豪华精选(The Luxury Collection®)、瑞吉酒店及度假酒店(St. Regis® Hotels & Resorts)、威斯汀酒店及度假酒店(Westin® Hotels & Resorts)、W 酒店(W Hotels)和福朋喜来登(Four Points® by Sheraton)。

作为喜达屋酒店及度假酒店集团旗下最大的酒店品牌，喜来登为从阿根廷到津巴布韦各地的商务旅客和度假旅客的需求提供卓越服务。喜来登员工致力于充分发挥自身经验，为旅客带来舒适与便利并最终与旅客建立起密切友好的关系。

福朋喜来登集团酒店在客房内配有完备的商务和个人设施，以适宜的价位为旅客提供舒适的入住体验。福朋喜来登集团酒店的员工有着舒适而平易近人的个人风格，并提供力所能及的服务，让自助旅客能够乘兴而来，满意而归。他们竭力为旅客提供更为简单方便的住宿服务，力求让他们获得轻松、愉悦的入住体验。

热情、美妙、机智、消息灵通、热情欢迎。W酒店实现了风格与内涵的完美平衡，它重新定义并创新地推出了高档酒店的入住体验。W 酒店的员工将以不同寻常的独特方式来满足并超越旅客的期待。他们热情、善谈、开朗并且体贴周到，他们会给旅客带来轻松的氛围，让旅客赞叹不已，并展示出专业的态度和精到的视野。

向旅途中的新变化道声好……雅乐轩是全新的目的港湾，它是为旅客在旅行的荒漠中带来的一个时尚而放松的绿洲。雅乐轩酒店的员工对待生命中的任何事物都满怀清新而积极的态度，他们知道如何游刃有余、体贴周到地应付任何事件。

雅乐轩的员工始终保持欢快的个性，但又不失稳重的内涵，坚持不懈地为旅途上的匆匆过客提供一个时尚、轻松而令人振奋的栖息之地。

豪华精选是拥有别具一格酒店及度假酒店的酒店集团，可为尊贵的旅客提供不同凡响的高品质服务。所有这些酒店(其中部分已拥有数百年历史)在国际上均被公认为位居全球最佳酒店之列。豪华精选酒店及度假酒店以其富丽堂皇的装潢、豪华壮观的布置、完美无缺的服务和最为现代化的便利设施而著称。豪华精选酒店及度假酒店的员工致力于为高品位的尊贵客户提供远远超出其期望的卓越服务。

艾美酒店在欧洲、美洲、亚太地区、中东和非洲的世界顶级旅游胜地提供带有法国风情的独特欧式入住体验。艾美酒店的员工友好和善、性情开朗，他们竭诚努力，力求让每位旅客都能获得愉快而积极的体验。他们时刻准备着付出额外的努力，试图提供超越客户期待的卓越服务。

element 酒店的灵感来自于威斯汀，是一家与众不同，结合了现代设计、精巧构思、高效空间利用和高档设施的酒店，主要面向长期住客。element 采用了极为现代化的理念，采用干净清爽并有效利用空间的直觉化设计，有助于提高旅客的工作效率，并带来一切尽在掌控之中的感觉。element 酒店员工的使命如下：他们热衷创新，致力于寻求协助旅客实现其固有潜能的途径。他们彼此尊重、互相激励并全力以赴，是 element 酒店实现营造良好环境、焕发旅客活力这一目标不可或缺的一部分。

威斯汀酒店及度假酒店凭借其轻松愉悦的风格和亲切优雅的态度重新诠释了高效服务的内涵，从而确保旅客获得难忘的入住体验。对于那些重视高标准服务的旅客而言，每家威斯汀酒店都意味着一个宁静的栖息港湾以及不同凡响的生活方式。威斯汀酒店配有天梦之床(Heavenly Bed®)和天梦之浴(Heavenly Bath®)等超豪华设施，其员工致力于在“恢复活力之旅”中为旅客“缓解压力”并提供服务。

在全球豪华酒店中，在入住标准和优雅程度方面享有顶级卓越水准声誉的酒店屈指可数。瑞吉酒店及度假酒店则是这些超高档酒店中的佼佼者。瑞吉酒店向旅客展示出永恒传世的高雅格调，坚定不移的尊贵品位、关怀备至的悉心照料和不亢不卑的得体态度，成为旅客别无他选的独特栖息之所。酒店内无可挑剔的员工能提供远超其职责范围的服务，并致力于从每一个细节着手确保为旅客带来尽善尽美的舒适享受。